Wicked Cool Sustainable Solutions for the EARTH

Written and Illustrated by Becky Johnson
Edited by Donna Tarbania

Syracuse Cultural Workers
Syracuse, New York, USA

Contents

Key

- * **Definition is in glossary**
- ☆ **Activity in back related to page**
- [R] **Resource(s) in back related to page**

Sustainable Solutions

We humans have caused many problems for ourselves. We have some bad habits, like messing up our environment, fighting over the things the Earth provides for us, and not considering the long-term consequences of the things we do. While many of us are trying to find solutions to fix our problems, some solutions are better than others. A sustainable solution* is one that considers the connections between the people, animals and plants that share a home on Earth. It allows humans to meet their needs in the present without compromising the ability of future generations to meet their own needs.

An example of a problem is **TOO MUCH TRASH**. One idea for a solution is to dig a big hole, put the trash in it, and cover it with dirt! This is called a landfill. Landfills are **NOT** sustainable because nasty poisonous chemicals leak into surrounding land and water. Besides, it does not solve the problem of too much trash. Someone else's idea is to recycle. Recycling is good because it helps us reuse things. But the best, sustainable solution would also help us not make so much trash in the first place!

This book helps you to be your own problem-solver. Start to look at the world around you. What are the problems you see? How do you think you could solve them in ways that will leave the world better than you found it?

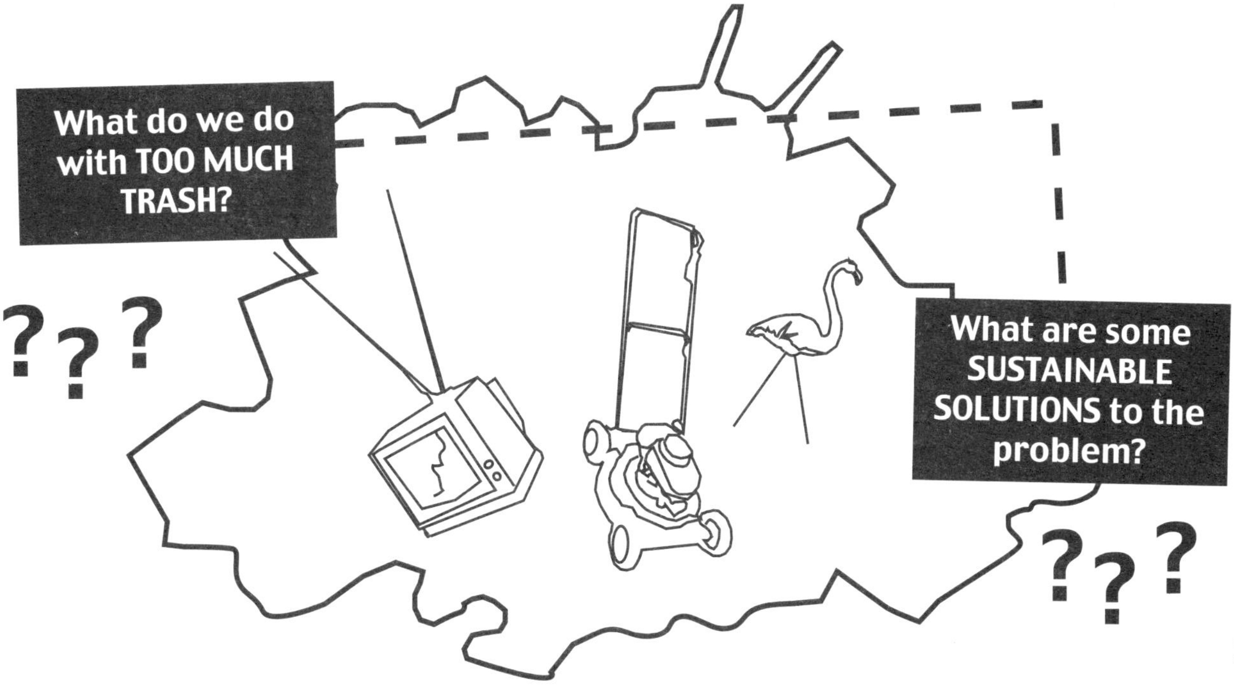

Use your bRain!!! What is the worst problem in the world that you can think of? How does this problem affect the environment? the animals? the people? How does this problem affect YOU? Can you draw a solution to the problem? What can YOU do?

TROUBLE WITH THE 3 RS!

Recycling is important but everyone forgets to **REDUCE** and **REUSE** first! To **REDUCE** what you use think about how much you really need of something. For example, do you really **NEED** that super-awesome-cool toy? Do you have **ENOUGH** toys? When you **REDUCE** how much you buy and use you **REDUCE** how many resources you use from the Earth.

To **REUSE** means using something again and again. If you have a lunch box or canvas bag, you can **REUSE** it to carry your lunch everyday.

REDUCE and **REUSE FIRST**! Then Recycle!

THINKING ABOUT PAPER:
If it's NOT *postconsumer**, it's NOT *recycled!*

When paper goes to a consumer (you) and is then recycled, it is called ***POSTCONSUMER RECYCLED PAPER.*** It's important to make sure the paper that you buy is REALLY recycled! ***CHECK FOR THE POSTCONSUMER CONTENT!*** You often see just the word "recycled" on paper products. This means that trimmings and other leftovers in the paper mill were added back into the slurry*. It doesn't mean that the paper was ever used outside the mill by a consumer. Does this sound like recycling to you?!

Finally, big companies sometimes call paper "recyclable" to try to get us to buy their product or to make us think they are really concerned about recycling and the environment when they are not. ***ALL PAPER IS RECYCLABLE!***

Your paper in this bin will become postconsumer waste and will be used to make new paper. Draw you and your friends recycling paper!

Keep the cycle GOING!

Paper making from recycled materials!

adapted from www.tappi.org/paperu/art_class/makingPaper.htm

What you will need:

- paper scraps
- warm water
- screen
- newspapers, towels
- a tub (larger than screen)
- any pieces of wool, sparkles, etc. to add to paper
- blender or food processor

What you do:

1) Tear up 4 cups of paper scraps to about stamp size and put in the tub. Add 1-2 cups warm water to the tub. Add sparkles, wool, etc. This mush is called pulp!

2) Process pulp in a food processor until you have a smooth consistency. Pour the mixture back into the tub. Add more water until the tub is half full. This watery mixture is called a slurry.

3) Place the screen in the tub. Strain the slurry through the screen until you get a layer of the desired thickness on the screen. Look for holes and lighter areas. If you don't fill the entire screen, your paper will have rough edges. Use a ruler to make straight edges.

4) Gently flip the screen over onto the newspaper. Put more newspaper and towels on top of the new paper.

5) Cover with heavy books, or other weight for 24 hours. Peel off paper and let dry a little more. DONE!

We found this perfectly good chair

in the TRASH and FIXED IT!

Help me decorate it!

Someone may really want or need the old stuff you think should be thrown away. Think about donating your unwanted things to a shelter or thrift store!

 Earth Day is the 22nd of April! Are you doing anything to celebrate?

We bring our own bags when we shop for food. Plastic bags are made from oil and paper bags are made from beautiful trees. Before store clerks put what you buy in these bags, you can say, "I don't need a bag, thanks! I brought my own!"

Can you draw some food?

FOOD! NOT LAWNS!
GROW A GARDEN INSTEAD OF GRASS!

Mom helps us plant a community garden in an empty lot. A community garden is a place where people who may not have space for a garden of their own can grow food in a plot. Part of the food in our plot will go to the local Food Not Bombs*, which feeds the hungry and says “no” to war! Gardening allows us to get great-tasting, fresh organic food. Our neighbors in the highrise are growing tomatoes and greens in containers on their balconies and rooftops. This work is tons of fun!

Composting is when you take fruit and veggie food scraps that normally go in the garbage and place them in a pile. It naturally will decay into organic matter that adds nutrients to the soil.

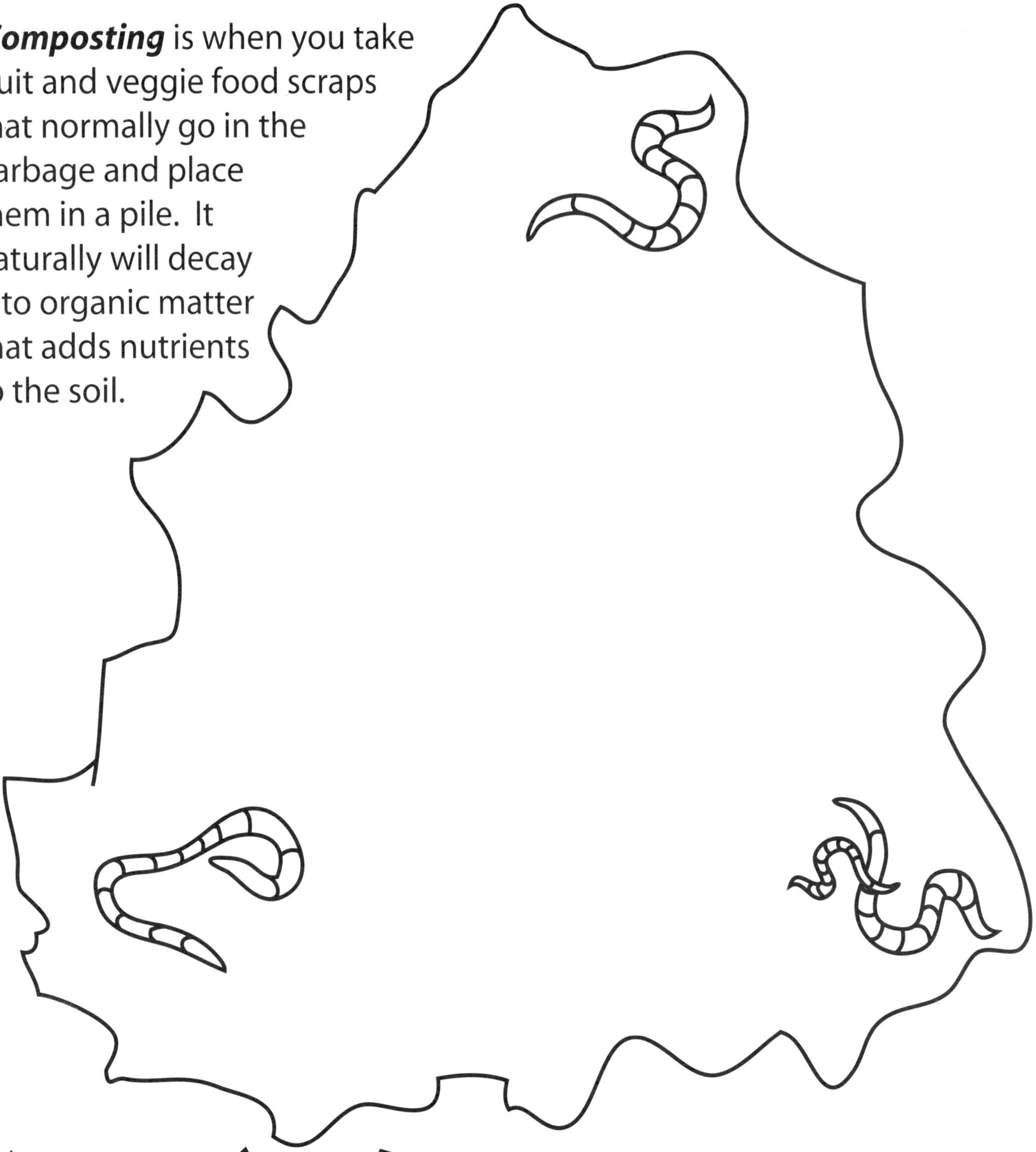

Vermiculture...

is worm composting. That means worms eat your food garbage (like banana peels) and turn it into nice rich soil that's great for growing vegetables and flowers. It helps to make landfills smaller and it's natural recycling! Draw some yummy garbage for these worms!

Our house is made of **DIRT**! It's called a cob house*. This is an example of a green* building. We also have a garden on our roof! This is called a living roof.

Can you draw a vegetable garden on our roof?

Genetically Modified Organisms

Did you know...

scientists are putting fish genes into tomatoes? Why do you think that is? Genetically modified organisms (GMOs)* are what some people believe to be a solution to problems with crops. They thought fish genes would help tomatoes live through a frost. What do you think? Can you draw what a fish-tomato might look like?

Go Organic!

Organic* means there are no pesticides or GMO seeds used. It is a way to grow food and live with the earth in harmony. Learn more! Support organic farmers. Grow an organic garden. You can help!

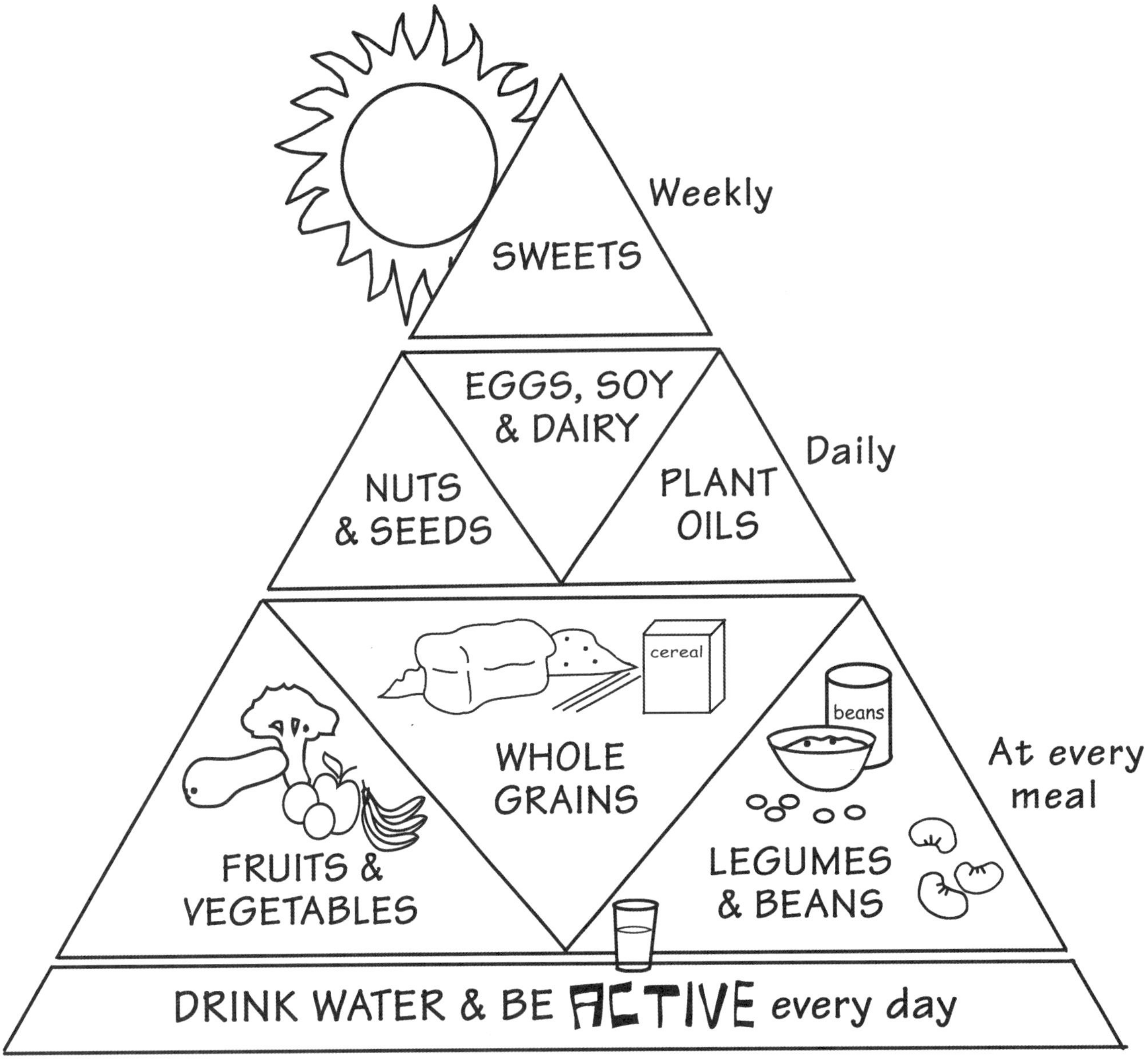

Vegetarian Food Pyramid

A vegetarian eats only vegetables, fruits, and sometimes eggs or dairy products.
A vegan (VEEg-in) is a person who eats plant products (fruits, vegetables, nuts, seeds) only, and often someone who uses *no* products derived from animals, such as fur or leather.
Why might these be good ways to eat? One reason is that by not eating meat or fish you can help animals' lives, the environment, and your own health. Raising animals for food is often extremely wasteful of land, grain, water and energy.
For example: to make a hamburger or milk, a cow eats lots of corn and drinks lots of water – the resources that support this large animal could instead be used to directly support many peoples' lives.
Do you know someone who is vegetarian, or vegan? Ask them why they decided to eat that way. What do you think?

ANSWER: 4. ALL OF THE ABOVE!!

Seed balls help beautify your neighborhood

www.seedballs.com

What you will need:

- 1/4 cup assorted seeds. Various wildflower & vegetable seeds can be used.
- water
- a bucket to mix in
- 1 1/4 cup dry terracotta clay finely ground
- 3/4 cup dry organic compost (worm compost works too!)
- water sprayer

What you do:

1) Mix the dry compost with the seeds.

2) Mix and blend this with the dry terracotta clay.

3) Mist water onto the mixture while stirring. Not too much!

4) Take a pinch and roll in the palm of your hand into penny-sized round balls.

5) Put seed balls in the sun to completely dry for a day or two.

6) Go for a walk and find old abandoned lots to throw them in. Water, or wait for rain to allow seeds to germinate.

Makes about 30-40 balls.

Dirty Kids

have more FUN!

Do you know what pesticides are?

PESTICIDES ARE DEADLY!

Many people don't like bugs (pests). But unfortunately, bugs like people's lawns and gardens. They gotta eat, too! Someone's idea of a solution to this problem was to create chemicals to kill all the bugs. Unfortunately, these pesticides (insect-killing chemicals) are poisonous, and not just to bugs! They are bad for kids' health and even bad for pets! Because they are sprayed on the ground they are also dangerous to our ground water*. Pesticides are a DEADLY IDEA!

Put up flyers in your neighborhood!

Get together with your neighborhood friends to do this activity. Make copies of the next page. Color them and put them up in your neighborhood to let your neighbors know you don't want pesticides used anywhere!

Flyer on next page →

Kids say 

Please don't use PESTICIDES on our lawns and gardens!

Where does your **water** come from?

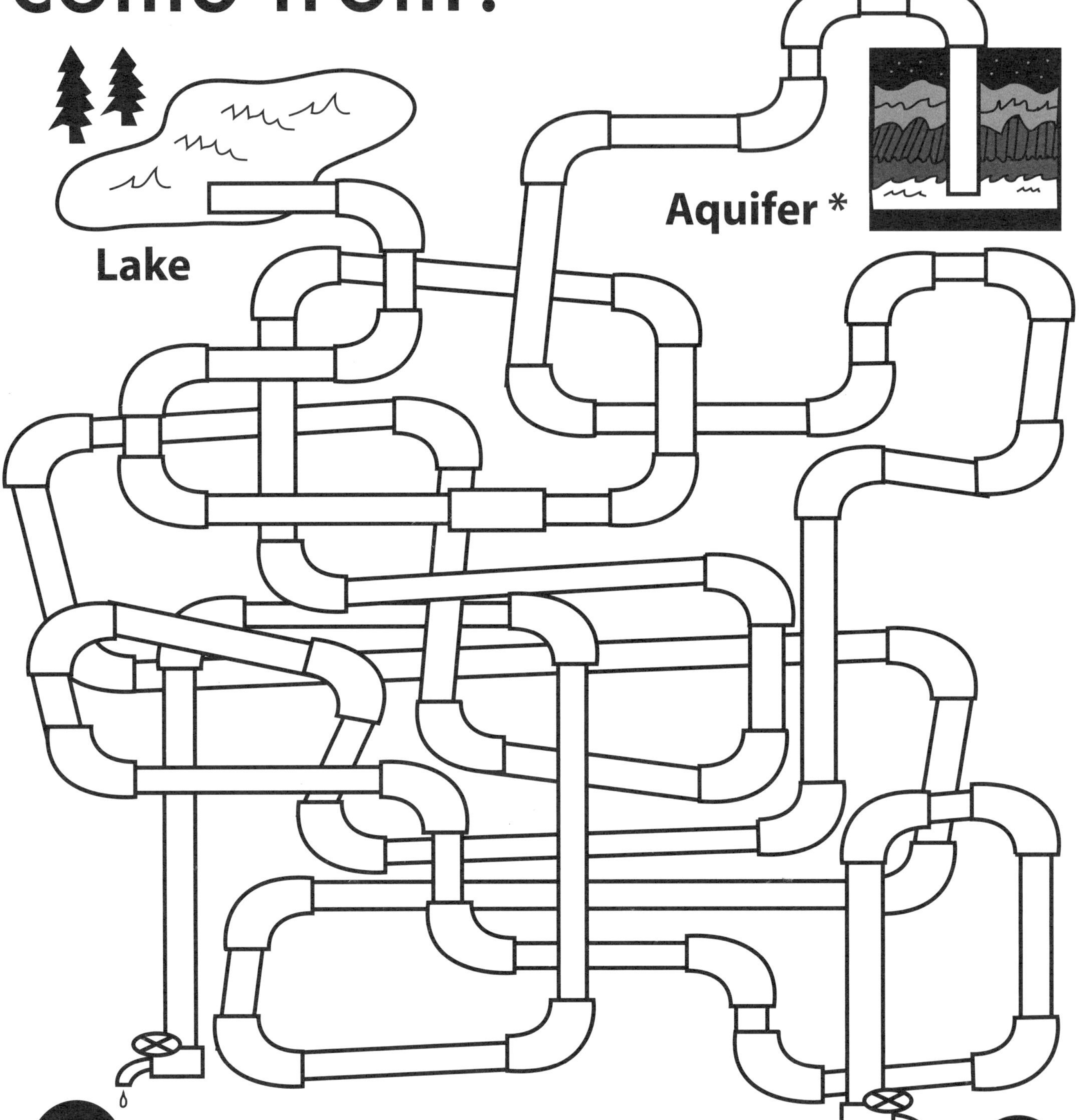

Water is one of the most important things we need to survive. Knowing where our water comes from helps us be aware of how to keep it clean. Pollution* can get into our lakes and streams as well as seep into the ground. Do you know where your drinking water comes from?

Take this short quiz to find out if you and your family are

USING WATER WISELY!

Do you...	ALWAYS 5	OFTEN 4	SOMETIMES 3	NEVER 0
Turn off the water while brushing your teeth?				
Put water in the sink when washing up?				
Keep showers to less than 5 minutes?				
Flush the toilet only when necessary? (Don't use it to flush tissues or things that should go into the trash.)				
Turn the water faucet off tight?				
Put water in the kitchen sink or a basin to wash and rinse dishes?				
Run the dishwasher only when it's full?				
Use a broom to clean the driveway or sidewalk?				
Use a turn-off nozzle on the end of the hose to adjust the water flow, and turn the hose off and on?				
Your subtotals:				

Your score:

If you scored 36 or higher:
Congratulations! You are saving hundreds of gallons of water each month!

If you scored 20-36:
Good job! You have made a start, and can use some of the ideas on this page to conserve* even more water.

If you scored 0-20:
Get started saving water now -- it's easy, fun, and it will save money, too!

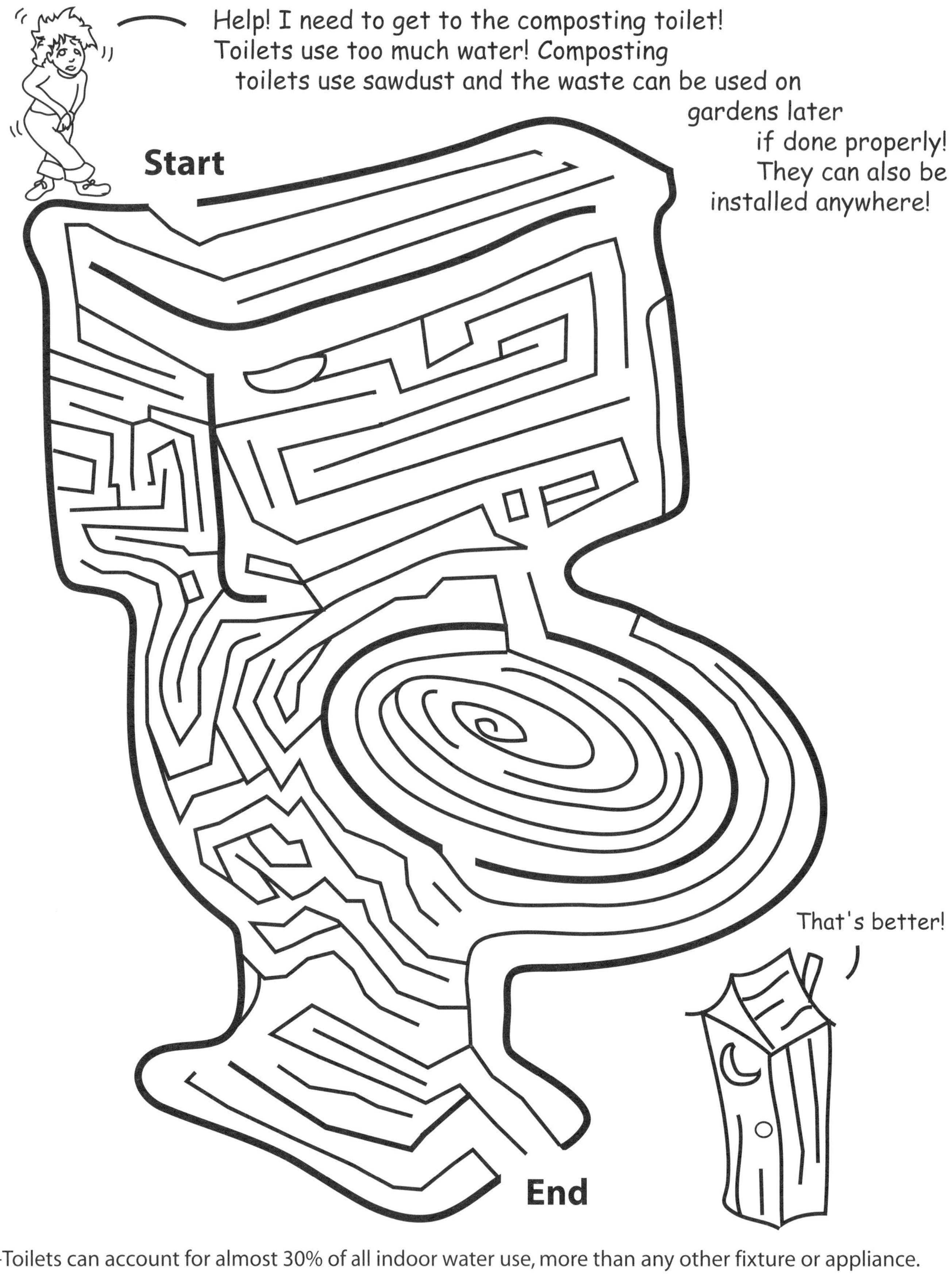

-Toilets can account for almost 30% of all indoor water use, more than any other fixture or appliance.
-Older toilets use 3.5 to 7 gallons of water per flush and as much as 20 gallons per person per day.
-An average of 20% of toilets leak.

Composting toilets! What a relief!

DID YOU KNOW?

The average person in the U.S. produces 4.5 lbs of trash in a day. That is about a person's weight in trash in a month!

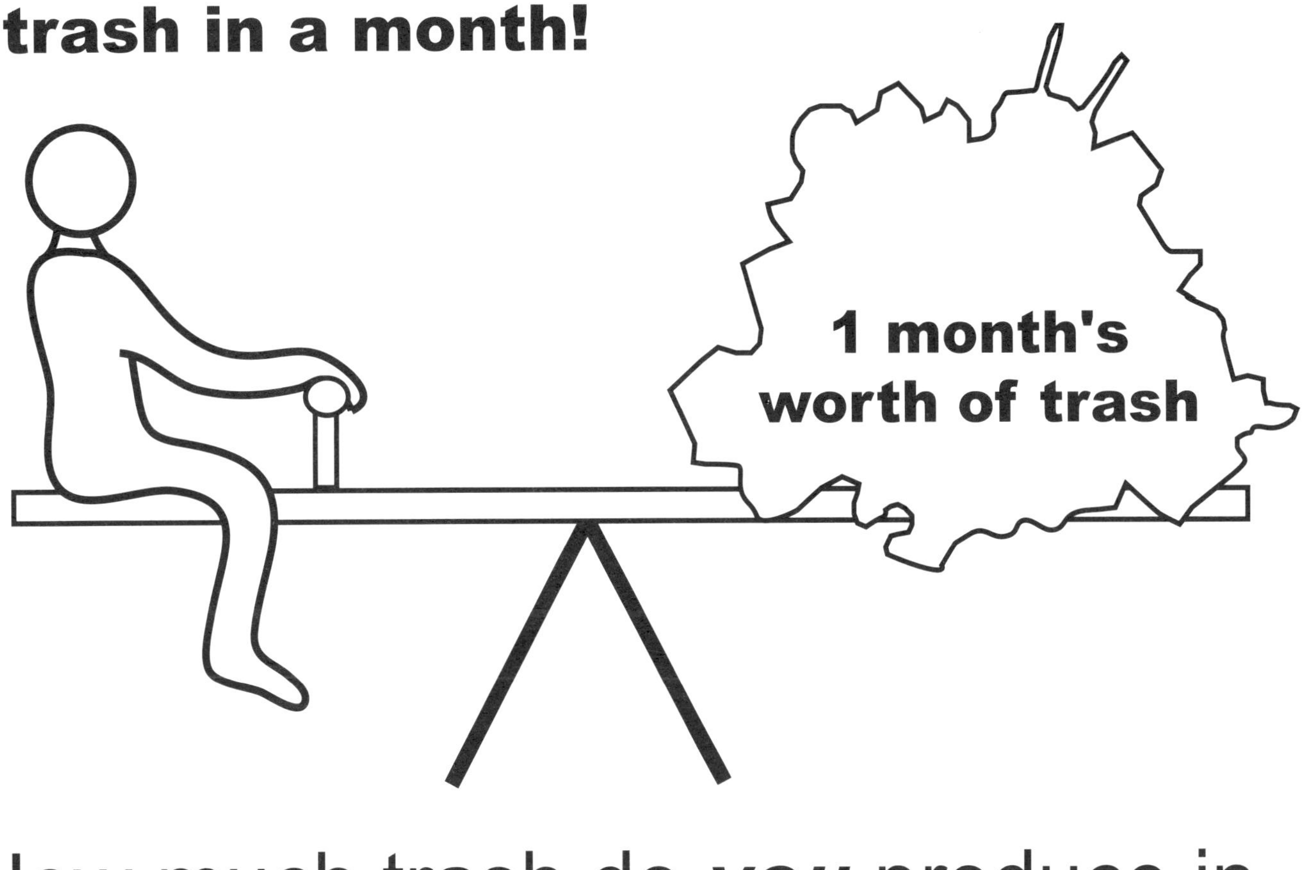

How much trash do ***you*** produce in a day? a month? a year? a lifetime?

your weight ÷ 30 days in a month = trash in a day
your weight = trash in a month
your weight x 12 months = trash in a year
trash in a year x estimated years of life = trash in a lifetime

Where does the waste go?

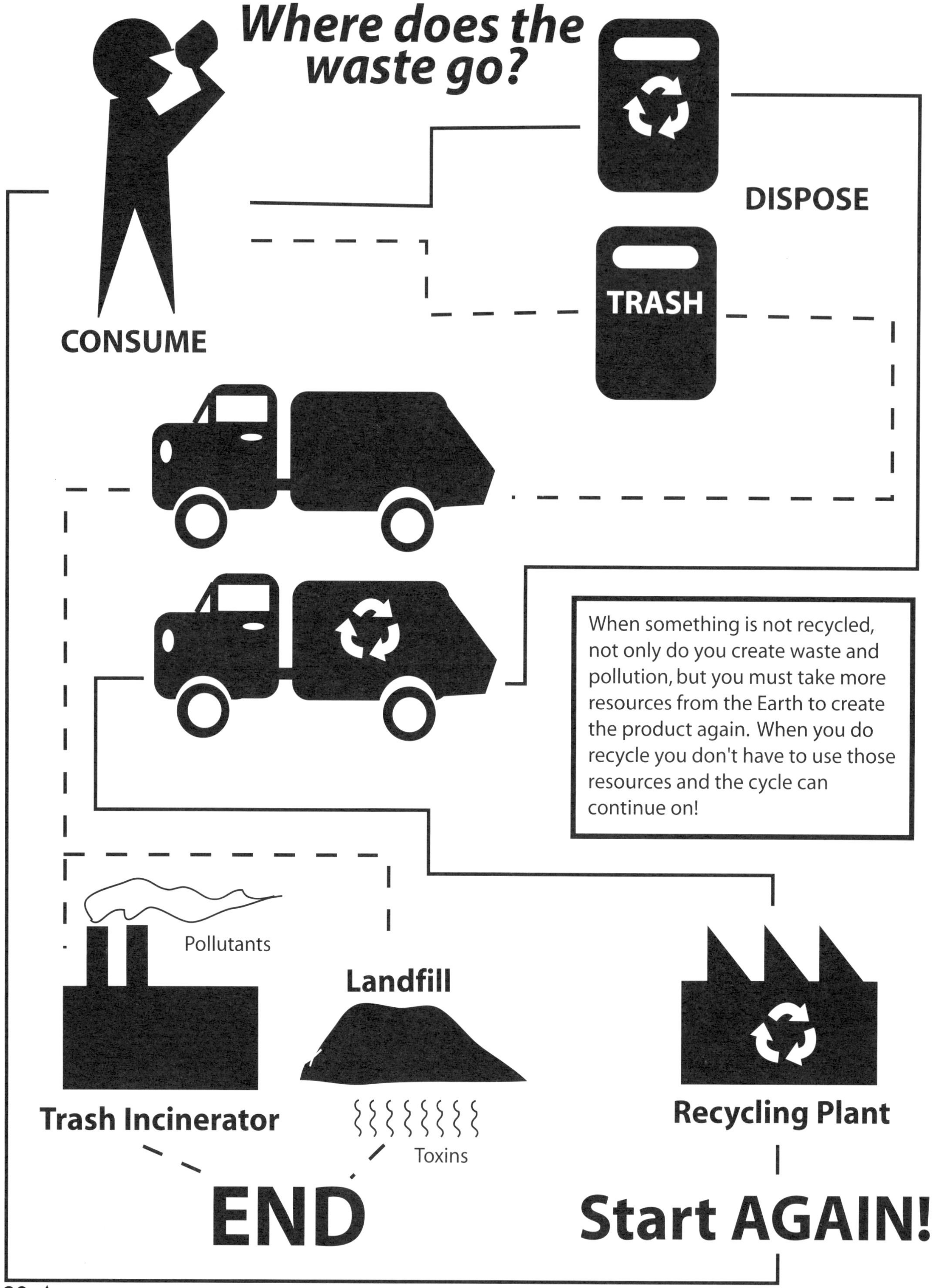

When something is not recycled, not only do you create waste and pollution, but you must take more resources from the Earth to create the product again. When you do recycle you don't have to use those resources and the cycle can continue on!

What do we know about the toy?

Sometimes a cute and cuddly teddy bear may seem like the perfect new best friend. But did you know that thinking about the label on a toy is **VERY** important if you want to make the world a better place?

why?

Well, what do the labels tell us?

- Where something is made
- What it is made of

think

What don't the labels tell us about the workers?

- Do the workers get paid enough?
- Is it a safe place to work?
- Can they take breaks?
- Are kids making the toys?
- Are the kids allowed to go to school?

What don't the labels tell us about how the toy was made and the effect on the environment?

- Is it made of stuff that is ok for people and the environment?
- Was the environment polluted when the toy was made?
- Was the environment polluted because the toy was made far away and it took a lot of fuel to get it to you?

That's a lot to think about! Do you really need a new toy?

FAIR TRADE

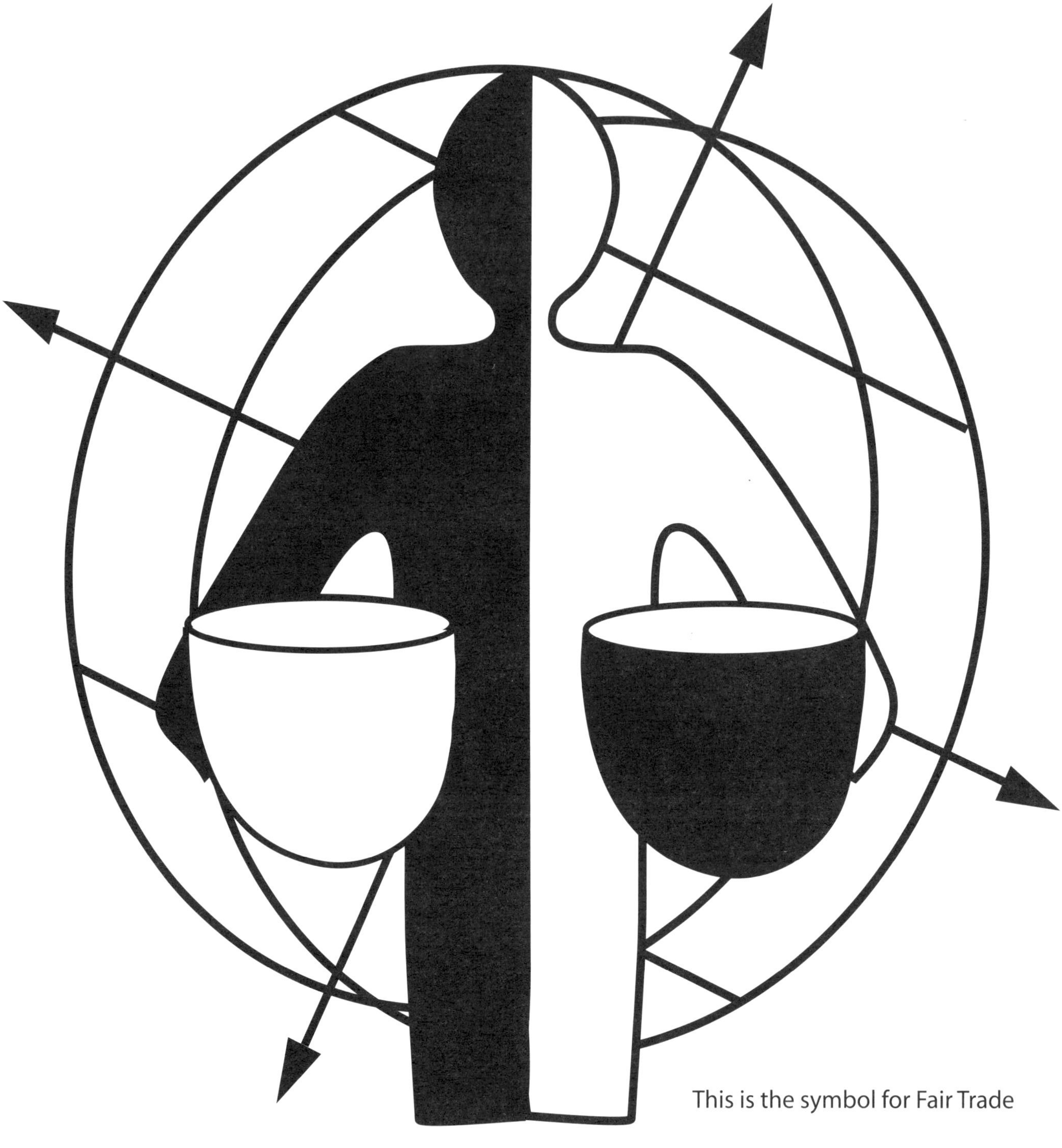

This is the symbol for Fair Trade

Fair Trade* means that the farmers and workers who produce a product received a fair price. A "fair price" means that they can feed their families and that their children can go to school instead of working. You might find the fair trade symbol on coffee, tea, chocolate and fruit. Start looking!

We are lucky to have such a cool grandpa! He is teaching us to sew by mending the clothes we got from the second-hand store. Next he's going to help us make stuffed bears from scraps of fabric! Do you know how to sew?

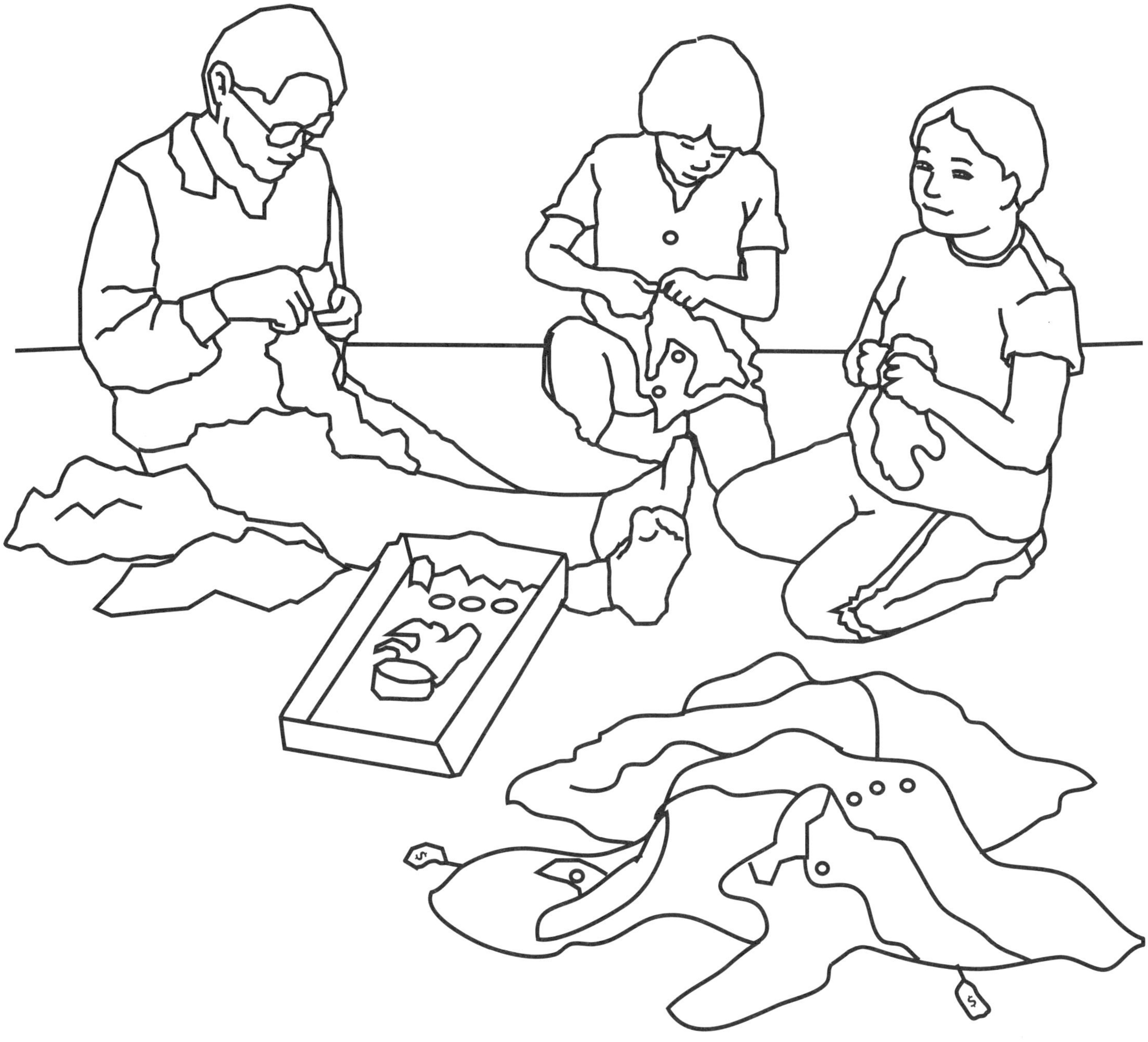

Have a CLOTHING SWAP* in your neighborhood!

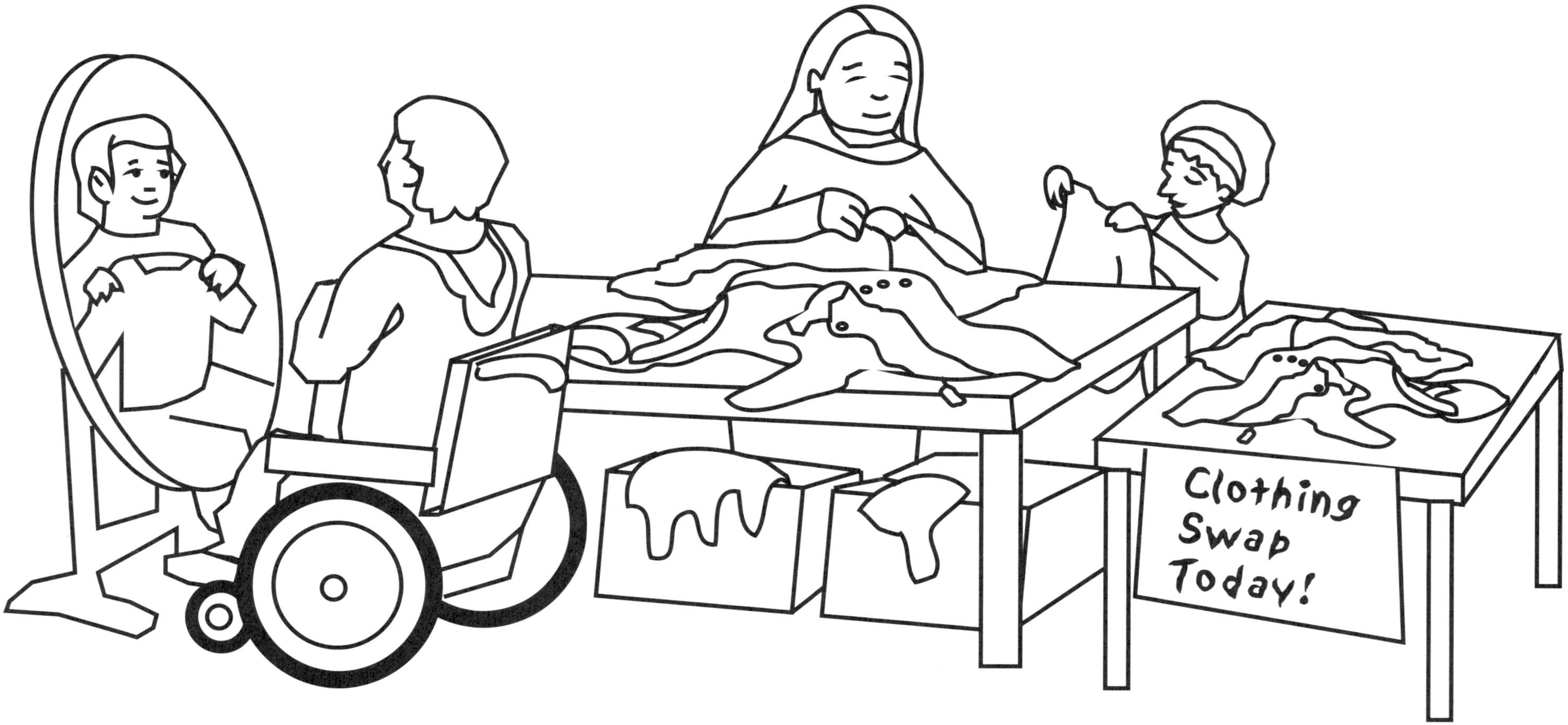

Reduce **the amount of new clothes you buy.**
Reuse **clothes from friends and neighbors!**

Which route is shorter?

(this one's easy!)

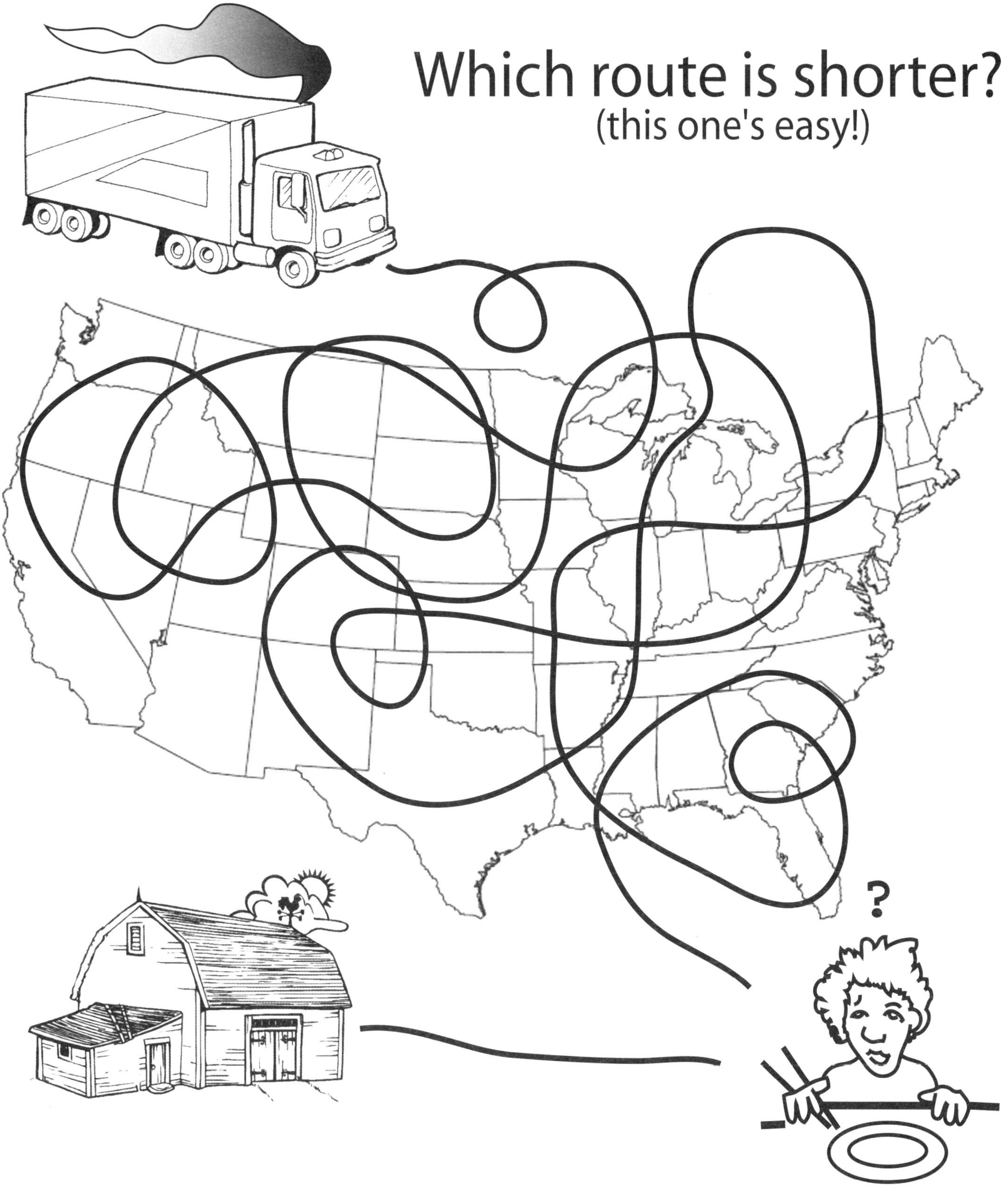

Some food travels really, really far on trucks or planes before it gets to your plate. That makes more icky pollution and uses more fuel. Buy food from local farmers! Grow your own! Eat the types of foods that are locally grown!

From here to there

CROSSWORD PUZZLE

ACROSS

1. Wheeled boot
3. Underground travel
5. Swimming cars?
9. Boating with the breeze
10. Horse and _________

DOWN

1. ________ your boat
2. Pedal power
3. Step on, balance and roll
4. "The wheels on the ______ go round and round"
6. Choo choo _______
7. Motorized bike
8. One foot in front of the other

CONNECT THE DOTS

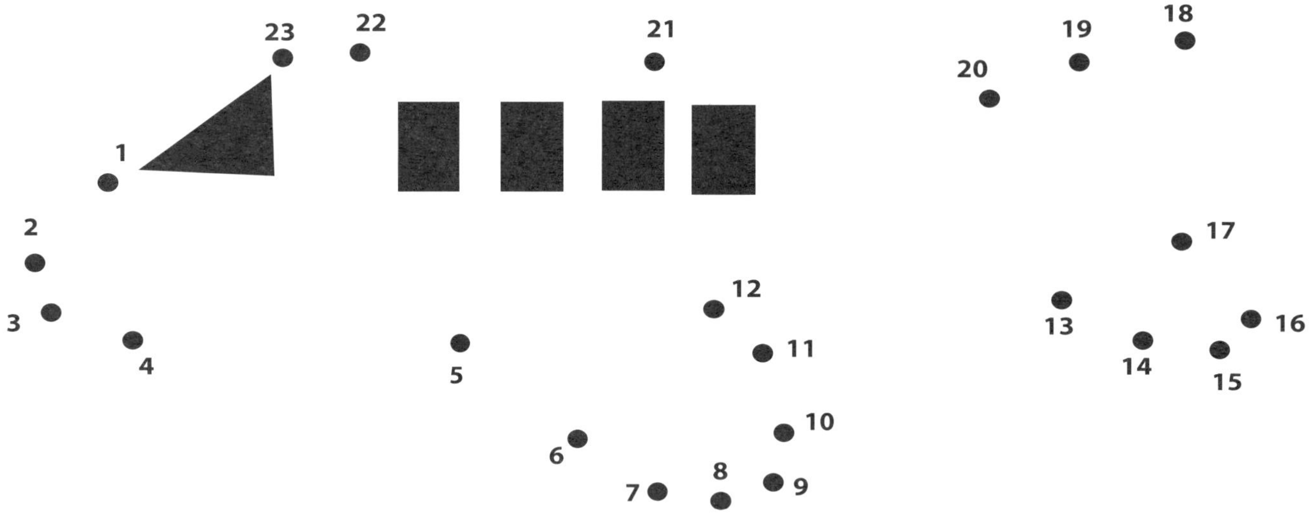

CONNECT the DOTS! You may think this is a good form of public transportation but it uses up a lot of fuel and makes a lot of pollution! Can you guess what it is?

Across: 1.Rollerblade 3.Subway 5.Car pool 9.Sail 10.Buggy /Down: 1.Row 2.Bicycle 3.Skateboard 4.Bus 6.Train 7.Scooter 8.Walk

SUBWAYS! TRAINS AND BUSES! OH MY!

A GREAT WAY TO GET AROUND!

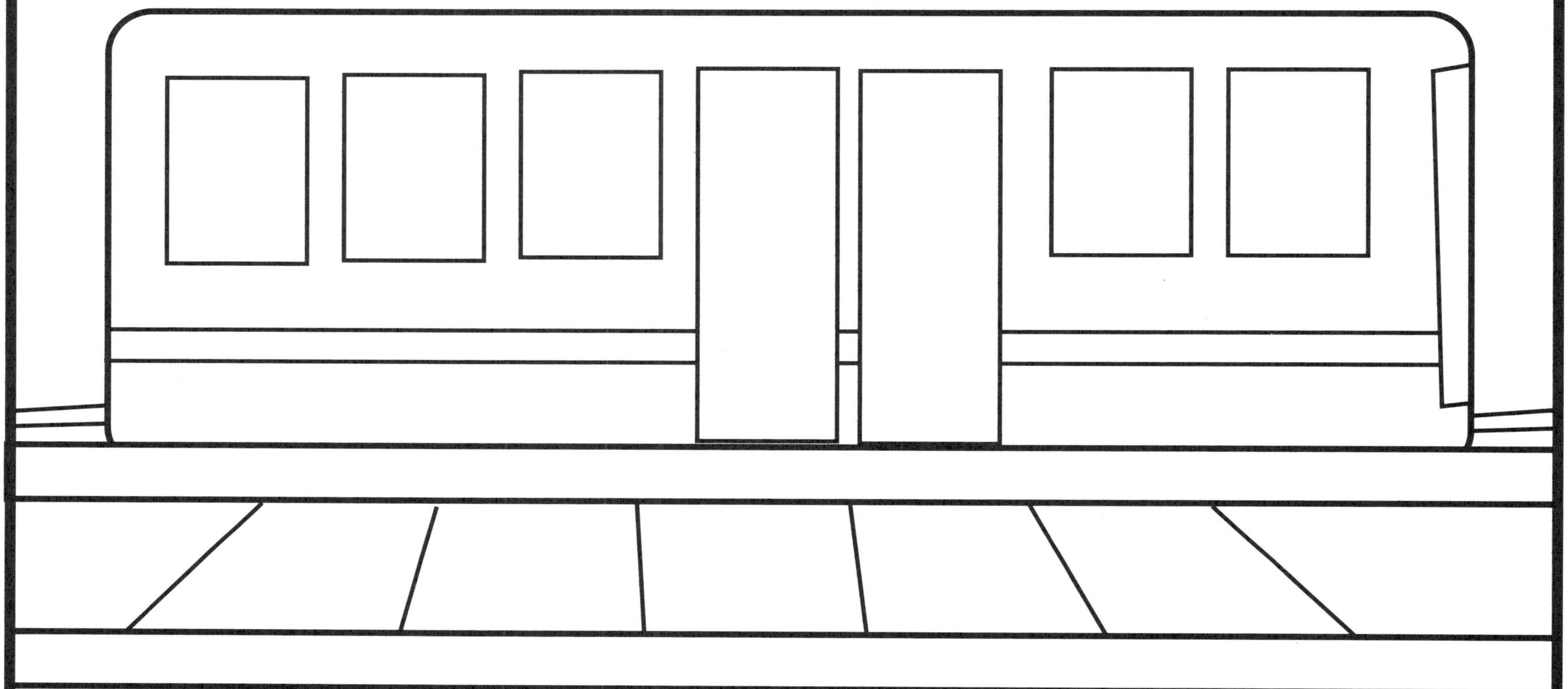

PUBLIC TRANSPORTATION* IS A GREAT WAY TO GET AROUND BECAUSE A LOT OF PEOPLE CAN SHARE A RIDE! LESS FUEL! LESS POLLUTION! LESS TRAFFIC! CAN YOU DRAW SOME PEOPLE RIDING THIS SUBWAY TRAIN?

I Like My Bike

Bikes don't use fuel, don't pollute and give you great exercise!
Where are the bike paths or other places to ride in your community?

Some buses and cars use vegetable oil instead of gasoline or diesel fuel. It's the same oil used to cook french fries and other fried foods in restaurants! It makes a lot less pollution and is using what would have been thrown away. The bus and car exhaust smells like french fries!

Draw a bus! What would you use to run it? Where would it take people? Would it be free to ride? What color would it be? What would it say on the bus? Have fun!

THE AMAZING ______________ POWERED BUS!

by ______________

We were Fools with FOSSIL FUELS!

What are fossil fuels? From the name, can you guess where they came from? Fossil fuels are found deep inside the earth, and they were formed from plants and animals that lived millions of years ago. Some examples are coal, oil and natural gas. The fuels are burned to release the energy that is stored within.

Here's a sad fact: it took the Earth ***300 million years*** to make fossil fuels, but in only about ***200 years*** humans have used up most of them! We were **not** sustainable in our use of fossil fuels. Now, we need other ways to get energy. What are some ways you can think of? Draw them! Need ideas? What about wind and sun power?!

ENERGY TECHNOLOGY word search

WORDS

WIND TURBINE

PHOTOVOLTAIC*

SOLAR

HYBRID*

ELECTRIC BIKE*

HYDRO POWER*

PEOPLE POWER

A	R	W	P	Y	L	R	A	P	W	P	L
W	K	E	H	P	R	N	C	S	R	E	O
I	S	A	O	Y	C	A	B	D	E	O	V
N	R	S	T	I	B	L	S	M	W	P	E
D	M	A	O	D	U	R	P	K	O	L	M
T	I	W	V	Y	L	T	I	W	P	E	L
U	D	S	O	L	A	R	O	D	O	P	A
R	V	L	L	A	E	B	V	A	R	O	B
B	O	H	T	N	D	E	N	M	D	W	V
I	B	U	A	O	V	C	L	A	Y	E	S
N	W	T	I	D	A	D	W	R	H	R	I
E	L	E	C	T	R	I	C	B	I	K	E

PEOPLE POWER

WIND TURBINE

PHOTOVOLTAIC (SOLAR PANEL)

Use a Clothesline to dry your clothes!

Using an electric or gas clothes dryer uses up a lot of energy.
Why not use the warmth of the sun and the breeze of the wind?!

Our trailer is powered by a solar panel!

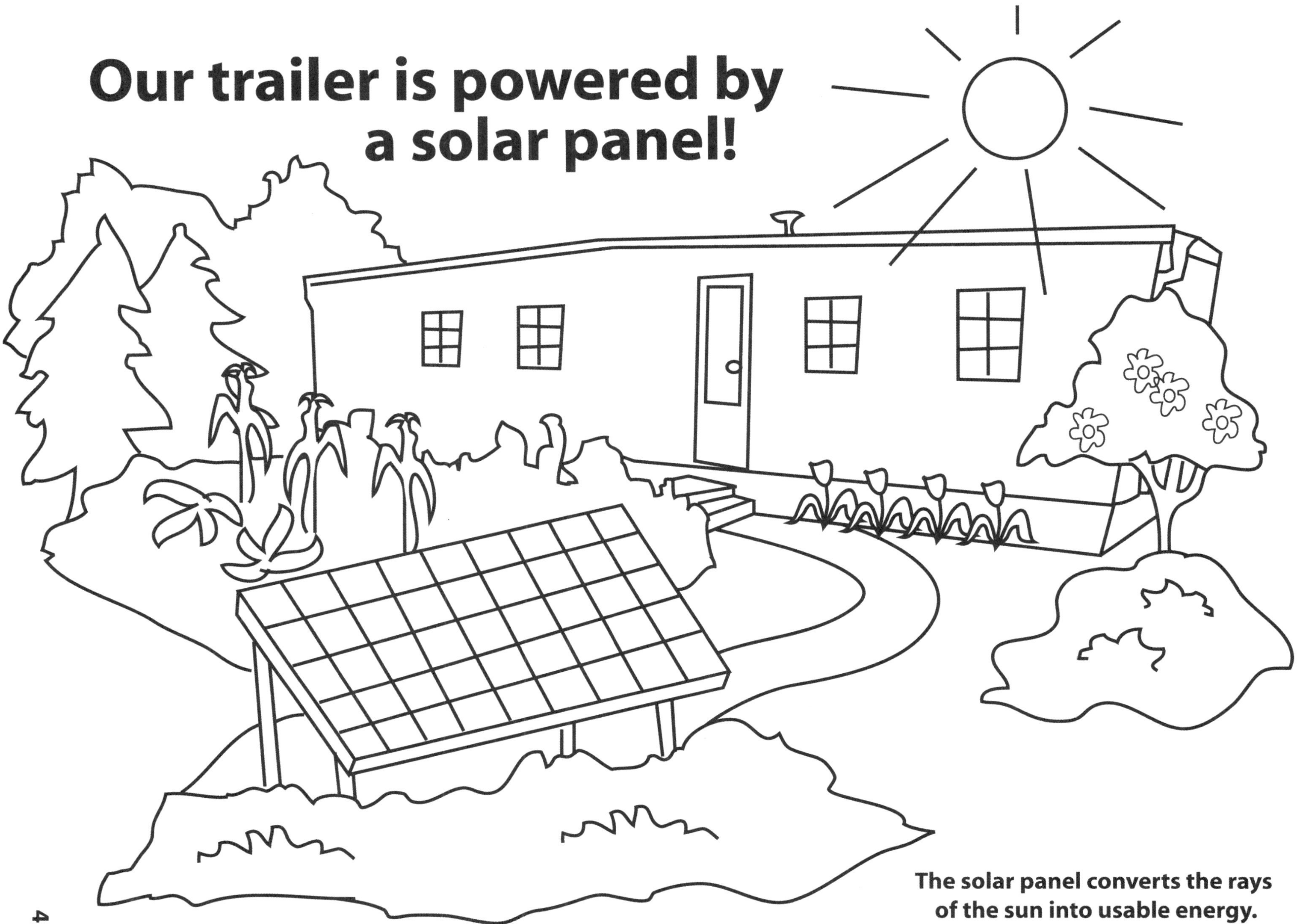

The solar panel converts the rays of the sun into usable energy.

Pop quiz:

Why use energy-efficient light bulbs?

(A) They use less energy than standard bulbs.
(B) They can save you money on your electric bill.
(C) They produce just as much light as standard bulbs.
(D) They last longer and don't have to be replaced as often as standard bulbs.
(E) All of the above.

Compact fluorescent bulbs

These bulbs provide as much light as regular incandescent bulbs while using just one-fourth the energy. For example, a ***15-watt compact fluorescent bulb makes the same amount of light as a 60-watt incandescent bulb***. Compact fluorescent bulbs last about ***10,000 hours -- 10 times longer than incandescent bulbs!***

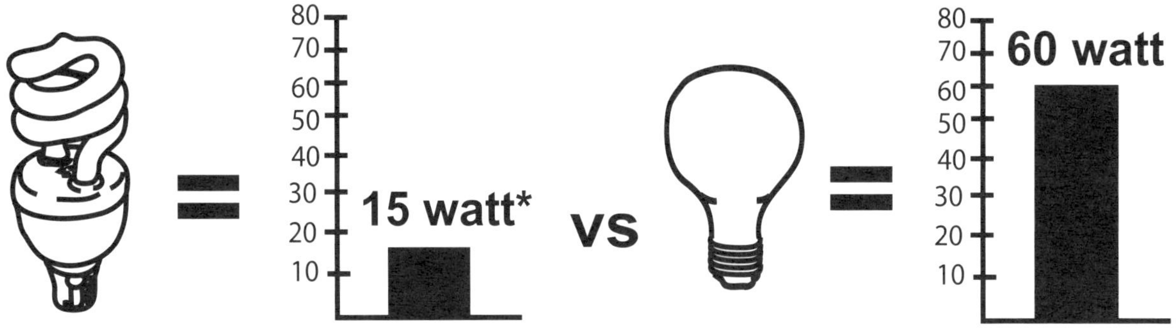

Compact fluorescent bulb — Incandescent bulb

Awesome Activity!

How many light bulbs are in your house? Count them and write down the number. Can you figure out how much energy you would save if you switched all of your bulbs?
Example:

# of light bulbs x 15 = watts for compact fluorescent bulb
# of light bulbs x 60 = watts for incandescent bulb
Now subtract the compact fluorescent bulb total from the incandescent bulb total = how much energy you would save!

Quiz answer: E) All of the above.

PEOPLE

People can create electricity by riding an exercise bike that is hooked up to a motor. The energy that is made is then stored in a battery. The battery can power small things like a 60 watt light bulb!

Fact: ***75 watts of power*** can be generated by an average adult rider at road speed in ***one hour***. Can you pedal without stopping for that long?

POWER!

WIND POWER
ROCKS!

Glossary: What do these words mean?

Aquifer is an underground layer that yields water. You must drill a well to pump the water out.

Clothing swap is a group of people, perhaps neighbors and friends, getting together to trade and share their unwanted clothes. Folks give away what they don't need or like, and others find new clothes to wear! This reuses clothing, and reduces needs for brand new items.

Cob houses are made of dirt. There are many ways to make houses that do not require wood. Houses are even made of tires covered in sand! They are called Earth Ships! (*see green*)

Compact fluorescent bulbs provide as much light as the more common incandescent bulbs, while using just one-fourth the energy. Compact fluorescent bulbs last about 10,000 hours -- 10 times longer than incandescent bulbs.

Conserve is to use carefully and wisely; to avoid waste.

An ***electric bike*** stores the energy you make by pedaling in a small, battery-powered electric motor. When you choose to no longer pedal, like when going up a big hill, you can draw on the electricity instead of pedal power.

Fair trade is when consumers buy products direct from farmers and other producers, at better prices, so that the fairest amount of money is given to the people who are making and selling something. Learn more at The Fair Trade Federation, www.fairtradefederation.org.

Food Not Bombs is a grassroots movement that shares free vegetarian food with hungry people and protests war and poverty. Hundreds of chapters operate independently to recover food that would otherwise be thrown out and make fresh, hot vegetarian meals that are served in public spaces to anyone without restriction. Check out www.foodnotbombs.net

Genetically Modified Organisms (GMOs) are created by splicing a gene from one thing--fish, fowl, plant, whatever-- and putting it into a completely different organism in order to give it some desired characteristic. For example, one of the genes of the Arctic flounder, that allows it to withstand cold, was put into strawberry plants, to help them withstand cold weather. The safety of such genetically modified food is an issue of strong debate today.

Green describes Earth-friendly and innovative ways of thinking. For example, ***green building*** is architecture and design that uses materials and techniques that work *with* the Earth to the building's benefit. For example, if you build with windows facing to the east, you can collect the warmth of the sun to warm your building. Visit www.globalgreen.org

Ground water is water beneath the Earth's surface, that supplies wells and springs.

Guerrilla gardening is when you plant food all over the place! Like the side of the road! Or in an empty lot! No guerrillas needed! You can use seed balls (p.20) to go guerrilla gardening.

Hybrid is a mixture of forms of technology. For example, a hybrid car uses both electricity and gasoline for power.

Hydro (short for "hydroelectric") power is when you use the force of running water to generate electricity. Small hydro power is a better example of a sustainable solution than large hydro power, which can be destructive to the environment.

Organic means using or produced with fertilizers of animal or vegetable matter, without use of synthetic fertilizers or pesticides. Also, free from chemical injections or additives, such as antibiotics or hormones. It is a way of growing plants and living in harmony with nature.

Photovoltaic (PV) means electricity from light. PV systems use daylight to power ordinary electrical equipment, like computers, household appliances and lighting.

Pollution is when harmful substances get into the air, water or soil.

Postconsumer products, like paper, are made from materials that have been used by consumers, and then recycled to be used again. "Post" comes from Latin and means after.

Public transportation is any form of getting around in which people share scheduled rides, for example, on trains, buses, or subways. It makes efficient use of fuels and energy and gives people who may not be able to afford a car a way to get where they need to go.

Recycle is to take useful substances or parts from things you are no longer using and transform them into something else useful. Plastic, paper, glass and metal can often be recycled.

A ***slurry*** is a mixture of water and bits of paper, or pulp (ground up wood or rags).

A ***sustainable solution*** considers the connections between the people, animals and plants that share a home on Earth. It allows humans to meet their needs in the present without compromising the ability of future generations to meet their own needs.

A ***watt*** is a unit of electric power, in this case a measure of the total electrical power a light bulb uses.

Wind turbines (windmills) use the wind to produce energy.

More Activities

p.6 Recycled paper is made in a really cool way! Find out if there is a recycling plant in your area and take a field trip. Take notes on the process and ask a lot of good questions. Use your research to make a display for Earth Day that will educate people on why recycling paper is so important!

p.8 , p.9 Is trash really trash? Have you ever seen something put out for trash that looked perfectly fine, or gone to the town dump and saw an awesome bike that only had flat tires? Next time that happens, see if you and an adult can fix it! Even if you don't need a new bike can you think of someone who does? Why not fix it and donate it to a thrift store where it can have a second life? OR Find an old chair and see what needs to be fixed to make it safe. A little wood glue might heal a broken leg. Once the chair is safe, decorate it! Pull out the paints and have fun!

p.10 Earth Day began as a national day of observance of environmental problems on April 22nd, 1970. Since then the idea has spread around the world, and people celebrate in any way that helps them remember that Earth is home to humans and many other beings, and in need of our care. It's a day for planting trees and grass and flowers, for cleaning streams and wooded glens, for honoring and connecting to our planet. Do you do anything special for Earth Day? Why not do something at your school or even in your neighborhood?

p.13 Community gardens are not only a great way to grow food but to grow community as well! Is there anywhere near you that people could start a community garden? Is there already one in your area? If there is, take a field trip and find out how it is run. Ask some of the gardeners questions about the community garden and why they are members. See if your family or school would like to start a plot! Maybe you could donate the food to a local food pantry.

p.14 Vermiculture See if you can set up a worm compost bin in your school or home! Do a little research to see how it is done. *Worms Eat My Garbage* by Mary Appelhof is a great book to get you started!

p.15 A cob house is a form of green building. Do some research. What are the different ways you can build using green building techniques? What is your favorite type of green building? Once you do some research, get out your paper and design your own green building home. Would you have solar panels? Would you have a living roof? Would your house be built of bottles? Have fun and be creative!

p.24 Where does your water come from? See if you can find out! If your house has its own well, have an adult show you where it is. If you get your water from the city, find out where it comes from. Find out how people in other countries get their water.

p.27 Find out just how much trash you produce in one week. How? Carry it around with you! Have a few plastic bags with you at all times. Anything that you would normally throw out should go in the bags. Don't cheat and throw it away! Now carry it around with you for a week. You may get a lot of funny looks and a few questions! Just tell people you are doing very important scientific research. At the end of the week weigh all the garbage. Was it a lot? What was the experience like? Did it make you think more about your trash?

p.28 Where does your waste water go? Do you know? If you live in a small village or the country, you probably have a septic system. Your waste flows into a tank in your yard where it is stored until a truck comes to pump it out. In the city, the water that goes down drains or is flushed down the toilet flows through a pipe into a sewer that runs under the street. The sewer is a large pipe that connects to even larger pipes that eventually empty at the sewage treatment plant. See if an adult will take you on a field trip to your local sewage treatment plant. Where is it located? Why do you think it's located there?

p.31 Second-hand clothes shopping can be fun! If you have never gone before, see if an adult will take you to a thrift store. Can you find any cool clothes? Anything that just needs a little mending? Have you ever mended (sewn together) anything before? Maybe a pair of jeans just needs patches on the knees. Learn how to mend your second-hand clothes. Sewing is a great skill!

p.32 A ***clothing swap*** is another great way to get new "gently used" clothes while at the same time recycling your own old clothes! Maybe a church or community center in your area has a clothing swap, or you can organize your own. Set it up like a garage sale with tables and boxes, but put out flyers asking people in your area to bring old clothes. Don't forget to set up a mirror so people can admire their new finds! Have fun and remember -- everyone likes to have a little something to go home with.

p.33 Food often travels far before it gets to our dinner plates. What are you having for dinner? Ask the cook about it. If it's spaghetti with tomato sauce and broccoli on the side, see if you can do a little research to find where your dinner came from. Read the label on the can of sauce. The tomatoes are grown somewhere! See if you can find out where the broccoli comes from. Once you know the places, find them on a map. How far is it from where you live?

p.35 Do you take public transportation to the places you go? If not, ask an adult to take you on an adventure. Map out your city or area and find some places that you want to go. The challenge for the day will be to take as many forms of public transportation as you can to get to all the places you marked. Maybe you can only take the bus. Maybe you can take the train or subway and the bus. Is there a trolley in your area? Write a story about your adventure. Can you draw pictures to illustrate it? Maybe you could even make a book!

p.40 Do you use an electric dryer to dry all your laundry? Could you hang a clothesline instead? Outside, two trees work fine! You can also get a drying rack that can be used inside and out.

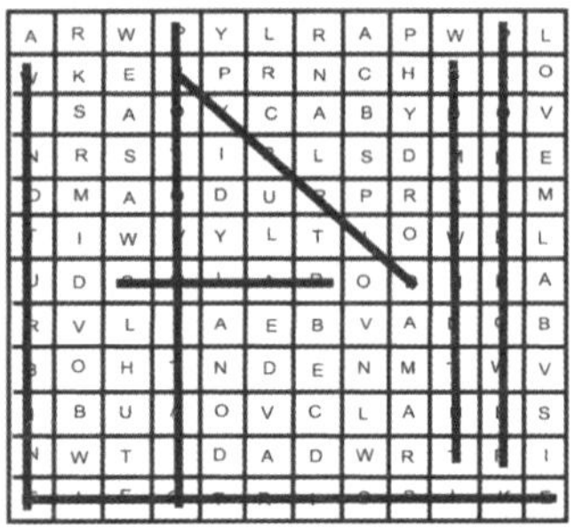

answers to word search p.39

47828807R00037

Made in the USA
Charleston, SC
17 October 2015

MW01714863

My Hero's Home!!

Written by Sherry Barron
Illustrated by Nick Adducci

Copyright

My Hero's Home!! A Guide for Young Children Whose Parents May Have Combat Trauma by Sherry Barron is published by Cru Military. It is part of the **Bridges to Healing Series**. The material and book structure of *"My Hero's Home!!"* were adapted with permission from "*When War Comes Home: Christ-centered Healing for Wives of Combat Veterans,*" written by Chris and Rahnella Adsit and Marshéle Carter Waddell (© 2008, Campus Crusade for Christ).

Published by Cru Military, a division of Campus Crusade for Christ, Inc., P.O. Box 120124, Newport News, VA 23612-0124, USA. For more information about Cru Military, please visit our web site at www.crumilitary.org or call 1-757-928-7200 or toll-free in the USA, 1-800-444-6006.

"The Greatest Promise" booklet information used by permission of The Jesus Film Project, a ministry of Cru. www.jesusforchildren.org

Illustrations by Nick Adducci

ISBN: 978-0-9863630-0-9
Printed in the United States of America

DISCLAIMER
This book is not a substitute for appropriate medical or psychological care for those experiencing significant emotional pain or whose ability to function at home, school or work is impaired. Chronic or extreme stress may cause a wide assortment of physical and psychological problems. Some may require evaluation and treatment by medical or mental health professionals. When in doubt, seek advice from a professional.

Hi Kids!

We want you to meet Cody and Carrie and their dog, Abby. Their daddy was overseas with the military and has come home, just like your mom or dad. This book tells their story.

Get out your crayons or colored pencils and color in the pictures. Read the story with your mom or dad. There are other activities, like making paper airplanes or baking cookies in the back of the book. Your mom or dad will help you with those.

Our prayer is that, as you read this book, you and your family will seek God, Who is able to make a difference in your lives.

Sherry Barron and Nick Adducci

Table of Contents

Dear Parents,

"My Hero's Home!!" is the first in a series of three books for children who have a parent dealing with combat trauma or PTSD. Each book is laid out in 13 chapters just like the book, "When War Comes Home: Christ-centered Healing for Wives of Combat Veterans," by Chris and Rahnella Adsit and Marshéle Waddell. Each chapter has related topics to elicit good conversation with your child, and uses concepts the child can readily understand.

The second book, "Helping My Hero!!" is designed for young readers in 4th-6th grades. The third book, "My Hero Hurts!!" is a study guide for teenagers. Each of the books have biblical principles that are crucial to any family looking for spiritual answers to the consequences of war.

"My Hero's Home!!" was developed for children in Kindergarten through 3rd Grade. The pages allow the child to get into the story as they color the pictures. The stories and activities will help them to ask questions they might not have asked on their own. Together, you and your child can better understand what is happening. You will see how God wants to show His love and care for you.

We hope you will enjoy the pages of "My Hero's Home!!" as you read, with your child, the stories of Cody and Carrie and their cocker spaniel, Abby. Their stories tell the many lessons they are learning about how their daddy's job in the military has affected the whole family.

Abby, the cocker spaniel, has her own ideas of what she can do to help. You and your child will enjoy seeing things from her perspective.

Each chapter has a Scripture verse, "God's Words." You could look the verse up in your Bible and read it in context. It is also a good verse to memorize with your child. The 'Key Words' section gives some vocabulary words to help your child better understand what is happening. You will find more information in the following pages about these words.

In the 'We Can Do' sections, the story shows how Cody and Carrie are involved in reaching out to their daddy to show they love and care for him. Those activities are described further in the Activities section of this book (pages 35-47). These activities are things you can do with your child.

The short prayer in the "Let's Pray" section is an example of how you and your children can pray in response to what you've learned in the chapter.

We know God used the verses, prayers and information to make a difference in Cody and Carrie's family. Our prayer is that your family will seek God, Who is able to make a difference in your lives too.

Sherry Barron and all the Cru Military staff

www.crumilitary.org

Foreword

Chances are you're holding this book and reading this forward because someone you love very much went to war and came home a different person. You also are feeling the effect of combat trauma.

Cru Military's "Bridges to Healing" project first focused on providing Christ-centered solutions for warriors coming home with spiritual wounds of combat trauma and PTSD. Author Chris Adsit wrote *The Combat Trauma Healing Manual* providing Biblical answers to address these wounds. Soon, realizing combat trauma affects the whole family and that wives face unique challenges, Chris Adsit, Rahnella Adsit and Marshéle Carter Waddell wrote *When War Comes Home*, providing factual information about combat trauma and PTSD. Its 13 chapters lead wives on a journey of healing for secondary trauma stress.

"Please get me something to help the children. They're getting lost." This was the cry of military chaplains from all branches when Cru Military asked, "How can we help you?"

With a passion to help military children, Sherry Barron used her experience as a military wife, mother, educator and author to write this book, ***My Hero's Home!! A Guide for Young Children Whose Parents May Have Combat Trauma*** *(K-3rd Grades).*

Following the 13-chapter format of ***When War Comes Home,*** this series of children's books also includes, ***Helping My Hero!! A Guide for Young Readers Whose Parents May Have Combat Trauma*** *(4th-6th Grades),* and ***My Hero Hurts!! A Study Guide for Teenagers Whose Parents May Have Combat Trauma*** *(7th-12th Grades).* The Christ-centered solutions and unique formats in these books will help communication between parents and their children.

In addressing the effects of combat trauma on children, this book fulfills a vision we've had since the Vietnam War. We saw these effects firsthand while in the Army, as Cub Scout leaders and while teaching in the Department of Defense School in Schweinfurt, Germany. As we studied the stresses on our military families serving during the Afghanistan and Iraq wars, the vision became clear. We are very appreciative of Cru Military, their financial supporters and Sherry Barron for making this vision a reality. We pray you receive spiritual healing from the Christ-centered solutions in this book.

Ron and Marcy Wheat
Cru Military Missionaries

1 ONE What Happened To My Daddy?

Carrie and Cody's family are so happy. Their daddy has come home from the war. They help him bring his gear into the house. After Daddy washes his face and hands, they sit down to eat supper. The children can't wait to finish eating. They want to go to the park. While Daddy is pushing Carrie and Cody on the swings, a loud motorcycle drives by. He puts his hands over his ears. All of a sudden he runs back home without Cody and Carrie. Mommy rushes out the front door as they jump down from the swings. The children run inside the house to see where Daddy is. Abby rushes to their sides wagging her tail. Both Carrie and Cody start talking at the same time. They don't understand what happened to their daddy.

God's Words

"I know the plans I have in mind for you, declares the Lord;
they are plans for peace, not disaster,
to give you a future filled with hope."
~ Jeremiah 29:11

Abby's Ideas

- Wag my tail a lot
- Lick Daddy many times
- Give Cody and Carrie extra love

Key Words:

- "**combat**" - Fighting in a war between two or more countries
- "**enemy**" - People who are fighting against us in war
- "**fear**" - To be afraid of something
- "**feelings**" - Being happy, sad, excited, caring and more
- "**pain**" - Hurting in the body, mind or spirit

(See pg. 50)

WE CAN DO:

- [ ] We will speak softly and hug Daddy a lot.
- [ ] We will make Daddy a great big Valentine to show him how much we love him (see pg. 36).
- [ ] We will pray for Daddy every night before we sleep.

Let's Pray

Dear God, we love You and we love our daddy. Help us to be good. Help our daddy not be afraid of loud noises. Give Mommy and Daddy a great big hug.

Love, Cody and Carrie

2 TWO What Am I Doing Wrong, Daddy?

It has been a month since Daddy came home. He doesn't talk to the children much. He rarely pets Abby. Mommy is always telling the children to be quiet. They are just trying to play. It seems like Daddy will never be happy again. Carrie stays in her room all the time. Cody just lies around the house and does not want to play with his friends. Mommy seems sad all the time too. When Daddy comes home, all he does is watch TV. Abby does not know what happened to her family.

God's Words

"Certainly the faithful love of the Lord hasn't ended; certainly God's compassion isn't through!"
~ Lamentations 3:22

Abby's Ideas

- Follow Daddy around the house
- Put my head on Daddy's leg
- Look at Daddy with my big brown eyes

Key Words:

- **"sadness"** - Feeling unhappy about something
- **"confusion"** - Not knowing what is happening or why
- **"suffer"** - To feel or see pain, death or sickness
- **"anger"** - Being mad about something
- **"battle"** - Fighting with someone

(See pg. 51)

WE CAN DO:

- [ ] Make Daddy some yummy cookies with Mommy today (see pg. 38).
- [ ] Draw a picture of the family and give it to Daddy.
- [ ] Obey Mommy and Daddy right away when they ask us to do something.

Let's Pray

Dear God, help our daddy and mommy be happy again. Help heal Daddy from his pain. Thank You for Your love.

Love, Cody and Carrie

3 THREE Why Are Daddy And I So Sad?

Two months have gone by.
Cody and Carrie's daddy gets up and goes to work every day. He comes home tired and does not say much. Sometimes he does not come home for supper. Whenever the children ask if he wants to go to the park, he always has an excuse. One day Cody asks his mommy if his daddy is ever going to change. She just shrugs her shoulders. Mommy tells her son she is thinking they should go to church. She thinks there will be some answers there.

God's Words

"He's the one who comforts us in all our trouble so that we can comfort other people"
~ 2 Corinthians 1:4

Abby's Ideas

Wiggle more and more for Daddy

Bring a tennis ball to Daddy to throw for me

Keep Mommy company when she is working around the house

Key Words:

- "**love**" - To really like someone a lot
- "**loss**" - To no longer have what you had before
- "**burden**" - A heavy load that is hard to carry
- "**sorrow**" - A deep sadness because you have lost something
- "**ideas**" - Thinking of new ways to do something

(See pg. 52)

WE CAN DO:

- [ ] Tell Mommy if you hurt inside.
- [ ] Ask Mommy what we all need to do to get better.
- [ ] Write in my journal book the answers Mommy gives me (see pg. 39).

Let's Pray

Dear God, we really need You to help us understand our daddy. Give us some ideas to make Daddy feel better. We all want to feel better, God. Thank You for Your help.

Love, Cody and Carrie

4 FOUR

Should I Say, "I'm Sorry"?

Mommy and Daddy had a huge fight this morning. Carrie ran upstairs into Cody's room. She was so scared. Daddy left the house after slamming the door. Mommy and the children have been going to church on Sundays. They have been reading good words from the Bible at night before bedtime. Last night, Mommy read from the book of Matthew about forgiveness. They learned when you do something bad, it is important to say "I'm sorry!" After Daddy went to work, Mommy called the children downstairs. She wanted to give them some special hugs.

God's Words

"If you forgive others their sins,
your heavenly Father will also forgive you."
~ Matthew 6:14

Abby's Ideas

Key Words:

- "**wound**" - A pain in the heart you cannot see
- "**weak**" - Not having the power to do something
- "**strong**" - to have great physical power
- "**forgive**" - To say "I'm sorry!" and when someone says "I'm sorry!" to you, forgive them
- "**choose**" - To accept an idea

(See pg. 53)

WE CAN DO:

- [ ] Hug Daddy more every day!
- [ ] Say "I'm Sorry" when I have been naughty.
- [ ] Make and give Daddy a "Chore Coupon Book" (see pg. 39).

Let's Pray

Dear God, would You please heal my daddy's heart? Help Carrie, Mommy, and me to be strong. Help us to love Daddy more each day. I love You.

Love, Cody

5 FIVE I'm Scared!

The family is driving home in their car after a day at the beach. Cody and Carrie have fallen asleep in the back seat. Suddenly, they awaken to the car's fast movements, the horn honking, and jerking motions. Mommy is looking back at the children to see if they are okay. Daddy is driving very close to the car in front of them. He is saying bad words at the driver. It seems the driver pulled too close to Daddy's car, and it made him mad. The children wonder if they will be in an accident.

God's Words

"The Lord ... is a safe place in difficult times."
~ Psalm 9:9

Abby's Ideas

- Wait patiently for Cody to play with me
- Make sure Mommy gets some extra love
- Sit by Carrie at dinner tonight and give her some extra tail wags

Key Words:

- "**rage**" - To be very angry about something
- "**tension**" - Emotional stress
- "**abuse**" - To not be treated in a good way
- "**safety**" - To be out of danger
- "**helpers**" - Anyone who can keep you safe

(See pg. 54)

WE CAN DO:

- [ ] Draw a picture of the best time you had with your family.
- [ ] Give Mommy some extra hugs today.
- [ ] Plan a family fun night doing quiet games at home (see pg. 40).

Let's Pray

Dear God, it hurts when Daddy gets mad at everyone. Please help our daddy go get some help so he can get better. Can we have our old daddy back again?

Love, Cody and Carrie

6 SIX Who Can Help Me?

Mommy and Mary, the next door neighbor, are talking outside about their husbands' work place. Mary asks if she can come for a visit after lunch and share ideas. Mommy agrees. She tells her to bring her children. They can play in the back yard.

Mary brings her son Levi, and he and Cody play soccer together. Mommy talks about the fright in the car that everyone had. Mary brings out a few copies of a booklet to share with Cody and Mommy. It is called "The Greatest Promise." They look at each of their booklets and open to the first page. It says, "This booklet tells about the greatest promise ever made ... and what God did to keep that promise." Mary tells them it made a world of difference in the lives of everyone in her family. Mommy thanks Levi's mom and calls the children inside. After snacks our neighbors go home. Finally, Mommy, Cody and Carrie sit down and read the booklets.

The Greatest Promise

- God loves you and He keeps His promises. Ever since God made the world, He promised to love and care for the people of the world.

Sometimes people break promises ...
But when God makes a promise, He keeps it.

People break their promises
by doing wrong things:
They forget about God.
They disobey God.
They hurt each other.

"sin" - God's word for thinking, saying or doing things that God tells us not to

"For all have sinned and fall short of God's glory."
~ Romans 3:23

- God kept his promise by sending Jesus. God never broke His promise to love people. He loved people so much that He sent His son Jesus to live with people and show God's love.

"Savior" - Jesus, the only one who is able to save or rescue others from the wrong things they think, say, and do (sin)

Jesus came as a baby,
and only a few people
knew who He was ...
God's one and only Son,
the Savior.

"This is how the love of God is revealed to us: God has sent His only Son into the world ..."
~ 1 John 4:9

Jesus grew to be a man.
He talked about God, His Father,
to everyone He met. Jesus told people about
God's promise to love them. Jesus showed people
how to love God and how to love each other.
And He always had time for children!

○ But many people did not love God, so they killed Jesus.

Jesus let them do this to Him because He was taking the punishment for all the wrong things everyone had ever done.

Jesus died so that all people - people like you and me - could be forgiven for doing wrong and could live in friendship with God now and forever.

Jesus died for you because He loves you.

"God so loved the world that He gave His only Son (Jesus), so that everyone who believes in him won't perish but will have eternal life."
~ John 3:16

"forgive" - to make a choice to excuse or put away punishment for wrong thoughts or actions

○ God's promise did not end when Jesus died. The best part was still to come!

God brought Jesus back to life! Many people saw Him and talked with Him. Jesus came back to life to show that He IS God. He has the power to help you stop doing wrong things and live the way God wants you to live.

"... I came so that they could have life - indeed, so that they could live life to the fullest ..."
~ John 10:10

Jesus returned to be with God.
Before He left, He made other promises.
Jesus promises to be your closest friend.
Jesus promises to forgive you for all the wrong things you've done.
Jesus promises to live in you
- where you love and hurt - where you feel glad and sad.
Jesus promises that when you die, you can live with Him forever.

- Do you want to ask Jesus to be with you now?

You can talk to God using your own words or a prayer like this:

"Dear God, I believe Jesus is Your Son.
Thank You that Jesus died on the cross
for the wrong things I have done.
Please forgive me for doing wrong.
I ask that Jesus will be with me and in me always.
Help me to be the kind of person You want me to be.
Thank You for answering my prayer."

"... I will never leave you
or abandon you."
~ Hebrews 13:5

"... Look, I myself will be with
you every day ..."
~ Matthew 28:20

- **"prayer"** - talking to God, either silently or speaking out loud

When you ask God
to forgive you and invite
Jesus to be with you, then
He **really is** with you and in you.

Now and always.
You cannot see Him,
and you may not feel different,
but Jesus really is with you!
He promised that He would be,
and He always keeps His promises.

Every day, thank Jesus
for being with you and for
helping you in your life with Him.

"But those who did welcome him,
those who believed in his name,
he authorized to become
God's children."
~ John 1:12

"faith" - believing what
we cannot understand;
trusting God's promises
and God's Son
no matter how we feel

"You are all God's children
through faith in Christ Jesus."
~ Galatians 3:26

7 SEVEN God, I Need You!

As the children sit quietly and listen, Mommy reads from the booklet. Cody asks if he can read out loud too. Cody and Carrie have been hearing some stories from the Bible at church but this little booklet is interesting. After hearing about Jesus dying on the cross, Mommy reads the prayer. She tells Cody and Carrie she would like to pray the prayer. She wants to know if they would like to pray the prayer too. They nod their heads 'yes'!

God's Words

"But those who did welcome him, those who believed in his name, he authorized to become God's children."
~ John 1:12

Abby's Ideas

Key Words:

- ○ **"promise"** - To say you will do something for someone and then do it
- ○ **"disobey"** - Not to do what you were asked to
- ○ **"rescue"** - To save someone from danger
- ○ **"choice"** - Picking an answer to a problem
- ○ **"trust"** - To act on what you believe

(See pg. 55)

WE CAN DO:

- ☐ Ask Mommy to buy us a children's Bible.
- ☐ Ask Daddy how we can pray for him.
- ☐ Make paper airplanes with Daddy and have airplane races in the back yard (see pg. 41).

Let's Pray

Dear God, we love You so much. Thank You for helping us know You better.
We pray our daddy wants to know You too.

Love, Cody and Carrie

8 EIGHT Who Are My Friends?

After going to bed and falling asleep, Cody suddenly wakes up. Loud voices are coming from downstairs. He slowly opens the bedroom door and walks to the stair railing. He sees his daddy and the next door neighbor sitting on the couch. Levi's daddy, Steve, and Cody's daddy are talking about the war. Steve is asking Daddy how he could pray for him. Daddy says he doesn't need any help. Daddy is saying he is mad at God because his friends have died. Steve tells Daddy he knows how that feels. He has pain in his heart too. He tells him only God can heal his broken heart. Steve tells Daddy more about Jesus while Daddy listens.

God's Words

"Friends love all the time,
and kinsfolk are born for times of trouble."
~ Proverbs 17:17

Abby's Ideas

Key Words:

- "**friend**" - A buddy you can count on
- "**kindness**" - Making time to help where needed
- "**patient**" - Taking the time needed when helping a friend
- "**mad**" - To be upset with someone's actions
- "**suffer**" - To be in pain in your body and heart

(See pg. 56)

WE CAN DO:

- ☐ Ask Mommy to invite our neighbors to a barbeque dinner.
- ☐ Write Daddy a letter to tell him '10 Reasons Why I Love My Daddy' (see pg. 42).
- ☐ Tell Daddy how much I love Him ... "THIS MUCH!" and hold out my arms as far as they go.

Let's Pray

Dear God, thank You for sending Steve to talk to my daddy. Please let Daddy know how much I love him. Help him go to church this Sunday with us.

Love, Cody

9 NINE I Am God's Child!

Cody, Carrie, and Mommy are sitting at a table in the backyard. They are reading a paper called, "This is Who I Am" (see pg. 42), that Cody brought home from Sunday School. The Bible is open in front of them. Cody is searching for a verse. Mommy explains what each of the words on the list means. Cody reads the verse from the Bible that explains the meaning of the word. Abby is lying at the children's feet chewing on a bone. Daddy finds them all in the back yard. He asks what they are doing. Mommy holds up the sheet of paper and reads the title to Daddy. He joins them while listening to Mommy and Cody. He offers to look up a verse Cody is having trouble finding.

God's Words

"But God shows his love for us, because while we were still sinners Christ died for us."
~ Romans 5:8

Abby's Ideas

- Rest my paw on Daddy's leg to get his attention when he looks away
- Stand up and snuggle next to Daddy for a neck rub
- Give Daddy extra wags when he tickles my ears

Key Words:

- "**chosen**" - Picked by someone for an important reason
  ~ Ephesians 1:4
- "**forgiven**" - To not be blamed for something I did wrong
  ~ Hebrews 10:17
- "**accepted**" - To know I am completely acceptable
  ~ Romans 15:7
- "**lovable**" - God cares a lot for me and shows it
  ~ Jeremiah 31:3
- "**connected**" - Joined together
  ~ Galatians 3:26

(See pg. 57)

WE CAN DO:

- [ ] Hug Daddy "Hello" when he comes home from work.
- [ ] Ask Daddy to help me look up the rest of the verses on the *This Is Who I Am* list (see pg. 42).
- [ ] Ask Daddy if he wants to play catch.

Let's Pray

Dear God, thank You. Daddy seems to be getting better. Thank You for our mommy who loves our daddy even when he sometimes gets angry. Thank You for our friends next door, who love our daddy and are helping him get close to You!

Love, Cody and Carrie

10 TEN Should I Pray?

Cody is spending the night at his best friend, Levi's home. Mary, Levi's mom, peeks in the door to say it is time for bed. She comes in to pray with the boys. Mary asks if Cody has anything he wants to pray about. He does not really know how to answer her. She tells Cody she and Levi pray for his daddy's work in the military. She asks him if he would like to learn how to pray. Cody is eager to find out what they do since both of their daddies work in the same unit. Mary takes Levi's Bible from a nearby bookshelf. Tucked inside the Bible is a paper they look at while they pray (see pg. 43).

God's Words

"But those who hope in the Lord
will renew their strength."
~ Isaiah 40:31a

Abby's Ideas

Key Words:

- "**prayer**" - Talking with God, either silently or speaking out loud
- "**danger**" - Could bring harm or pain to someone
- "**protect**" - To keep safe from danger
- "**strength**" - To be strong in any situation
- "**forgiveness**" - What you get from God when you say I'm sorry

(See pg. 58)

WE CAN DO:

- [ ] Copy Levi's prayer list and put it in my Bible (see pg. 43).
- [ ] Teach Mommy and Carrie how to pray the list for Daddy.
- [ ] Make a "*Thank You for All Your Hard Work*" card for Daddy with Mommy and Carrie (see pg. 43).

Let's Pray

Dear God, help us to be good children. Keep us strong. Help us to pray for Daddy every day. Thank You for what You are doing in his life. Let Daddy go to church with us on Sunday.

Love, Cody

11 ELEVEN How Can We Help Daddy?

Cody comes home from school asking a lot of questions. There has been a special speaker in his class from the military base where his daddy works. He was telling the children to give extra amounts of love to their daddies if they have just come back from overseas. He showed the children, on a map of the world, how far military men and women have to travel to get home. He explained how important it was for their daddies to travel so far away. He also gave the children a letter to give to their moms. Mommy reads the letter which contains a checklist of actions women might see in their husbands. Carrie wonders what is in the letter (see pg. 59).

God's Words

"We love because God first loved us."
~ 1 John 4:19

Abby's Ideas

Key Words:

- "**change**" - When something is different than the way it was before
- "**emotions**" - Feelings, such as fear, happiness sadness, and anger
- "**healing**" - Getting better than before
- "**argue**" - To disagree about something
- "**deploy**" - To be separated from the family due to military work

(See pg. 59)

WE CAN DO:

- ☐ See if Daddy wants to go to a ball game with Levi and his daddy.
- ☐ Ask Daddy to give me a tour of where he works.
- ☐ Make some "*We're Proud of You Because ...*" cards to give to Daddy each morning (see pg. 44).

Let's Pray

Dear God, help us love You more and more. Thank You for what You are doing in Daddy's life. Make him stronger and stronger each day. Help us show him how we are proud of him.

Love, Cody and Carrie

12 TWELVE How Can We Help Each Other?

It has been several weeks since Daddy came home. He still seems so sad and gets mad so quickly. Yesterday, he yelled at Mommy about the vacuum cleaner being on when he wanted to watch a football game. He said some bad words to her, and it scared the children. Carrie and Cody went into Cody's room and shut the door. Even though Carrie was crying, she calmed down when asked if she wanted to pray for Daddy and Mommy. The children were praying when the door to the bedroom opened up. It was Daddy. He stood there looking at the children with a very long face. Mommy had told the children to stop and pray whenever Daddy had a problem. They know God wants to help Daddy get better.

God's Words

"Don't be anxious about anything; rather bring up all of your requests to God."
~ Philippians 4:6

WHAT TO LOOK FOR BECAUSE MY DADDY IS HURTING

Daddy does not want to play. → Be patient. He will play again soon.

Daddy is tired when he gets home. → Let him rest so he feels better.

Daddy does not like loud noises. → Try not to play so loudly in the house.

Daddy can get angry. → He doesn't mean to be mad.

Daddy always seems to be sad. → He has a broken heart. You can pray for him.

Daddy has a hard time sleeping. → He is having bad dreams because of war.

Daddy drives the car too fast. → He tries to forget bad memories.

Daddy doesn't go to church much. → He is mad at God.

Key Words:

- "depressed" - Having a big sadness in the heart all the time
- "trauma" - A pain in the body or the heart
- "understand" - To have knowledge about a certain topic
- "truth" - The real story
- "broken" - To have a heart filled with pain

(See pg. 61)

WE CAN DO:

- ☐ Make a *"God's Promises"* poster to give to Daddy (see pg. 45).
- ☐ Tell Mommy you'll help vacuum when Daddy is at work.
- ☐ Ask Mommy and Daddy to go on a walk together after dinner.

Let's Pray

Dear God, thank You for helping us with our problems. Help us to say 'We forgive you' when Daddy says 'I'm sorry.' Help us to keep loving Daddy, no matter what!

Love, Cody and Carrie

13 THIRTEEN Where Are We Going?

Mary's whole family is at Carrie and Cody's house for a barbeque. Daddy seems to be smiling and laughing more. Steve and Daddy talk while they cook steaks and hamburgers. Mommy and Mary talk in the kitchen while they get food ready to eat. The children play in the backyard. Abby enjoys having more children to play with her. They toss the frisbee back and forth for her to catch. Daddy looks at his family and suddenly realizes how much he loves them.

God's Words

"Enjoy the Lord, and He will give what your heart asks."
~ Psalms 37:4

Abby's Ideas

- Make friends with the dog next door
- Fetch Daddy's slippers like Cody taught me
- Smile big when Daddy comes home from work so he will smile back!

Key Words:

- ○ **"transform"** - To change for the better
- ○ **"dream"** - To think about the future
- ○ **"depend"** - To count on someone to be there for you
- ○ **"goal"** - A purpose to work for
- ○ **"hope"** - To trust God that it will get better

(See pg. 62)

WE CAN DO:

- ☐ Ask Daddy if he wants to go on a bike ride today.
- ☐ Teach Daddy some of the songs we've learned (see pg. 46).
- ☐ Give Mommy a great big hug for making Daddy feel loved.

Let's Pray

Dear God, we are so happy our daddy is getting so much better. Help us all to know You more and more. Thank You for always being there for him. We love You.

Love, Cody and Carrie

Instructions for Activities

The following pages have instructions, templates, and information on doing the activities in the "We Can Do" portion of the children's pages.
The goal is to actively involve the children in activities that will engage them with their hurting parent, and demonstrate their love for that parent.
These activities may spark the imagination of the children to express themselves in their own way.

These pages are available at www.crumilitary.org/MyHerosHome so you can download and print them.

Chapter 1
What Happened To My Daddy?

Valentine

On the next page is a design to make a great big Valentine to show Daddy how much he is loved. You can:

- Copy it onto colored paper.
- Cut out colored hearts and paste them on a background.
- Color in the hearts and write your names on them.
- Use your imagination!

This design is available at www.crumilitary.org/MyDaddysHome so you can download and print it.

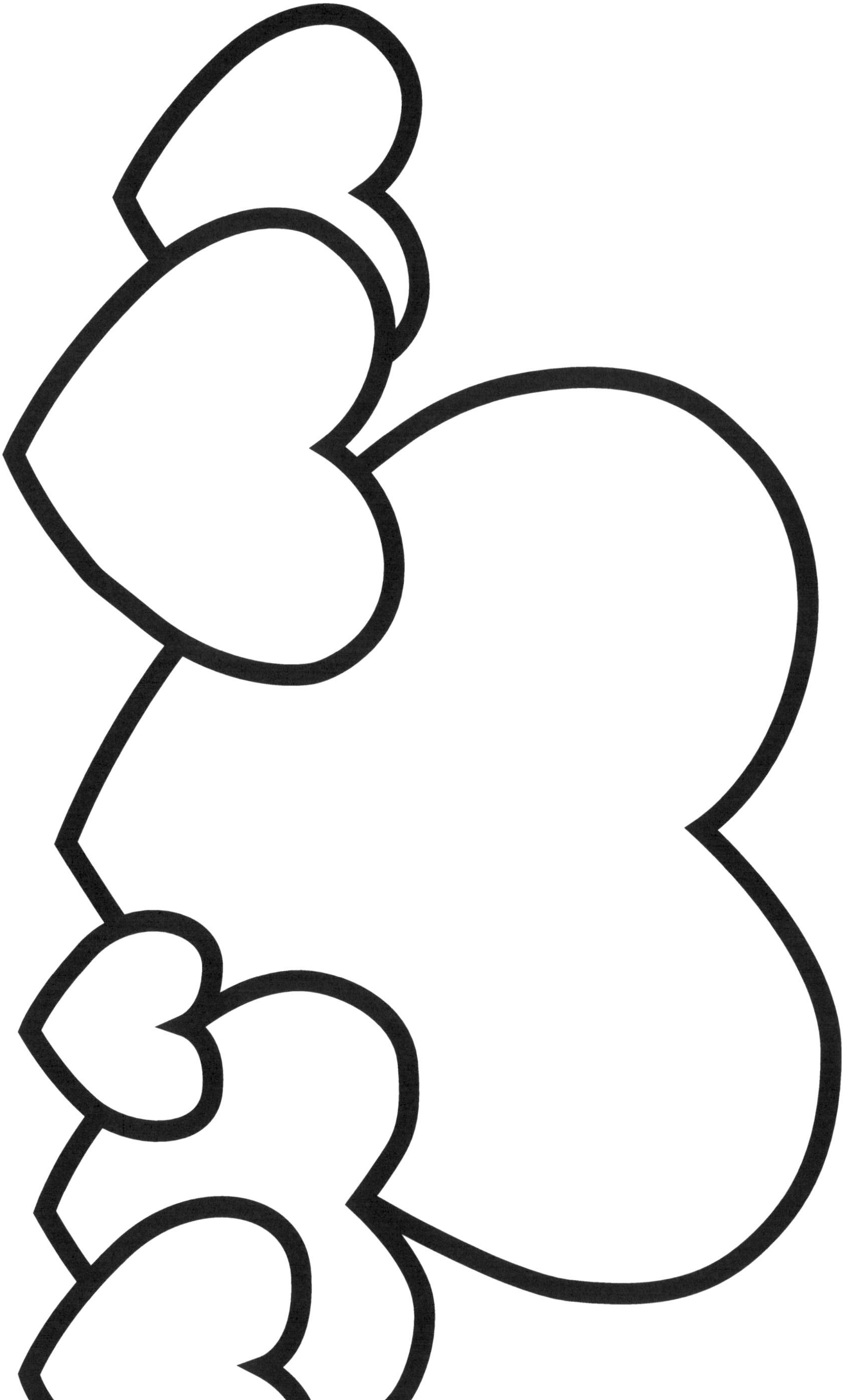

Chapter 2
What Am I Doing Wrong, Daddy?

Oatmeal Chocolate Chip Cookies

Ingredients:

1 3/4 cups of flour
1 tsp. baking soda
1/4 tsp. salt
1 cup firmly packed brown sugar
1/2 cup granulated white sugar
1 cup butter, softened
2 eggs
2 Tbsp. milk
2 tsp. vanilla
2 1/2 cups of uncooked old-fashioned oats
12 ounce package (2 cups) semi-sweet chocolate chips

Directions:

1. Preheat oven to 375 degrees F.
2. Combine flour, baking soda and salt in a medium bowl. Set aside.
3. Beat butter and sugars in large bowl until creamy.
4. Add eggs, milk and vanilla extract; beat well.
5. Add combined flour, baking soda and salt; mix well. Stir in oats and chocolate chips; mix well.
6. Drop dough by rounded tablespoonfuls onto ungreased baking sheets.
7. Bake for 9 to 10 minutes for a chewy cookie or 12 to 13 minutes for a crisp cookie.
8. Cool on baking sheets for 1 minute; remove to wire rack to cool completely.

Chapter 3
Why Are Daddy And I So Sad?

Journal

Let your child help choose a small notebook or journal book for him or her to use. Perhaps they could decorate it to make it their own.
On the first page write: **A Journal for (child's name)**
Write the following titles on separate pages:

I get scared when Daddy ...
I want to ... when Daddy ...
I feel better when ...
To feel safe I need ...

Help your child to think of the things he or she can write in the journal.

Chapter 4
Should I Say, "I'm Sorry"?

How to Make a Coupon Book

Fold an $8\frac{1}{2}$" x 11" sheet of plain paper in half. Cut along the fold line. Lay the papers on top of each other and fold in half again. Cut along the fold line. Lay the pieces on top of each other and fold in half. Staple the pages together on the fold line. Decorate the front with the words: **My Daddy's Chore Coupon Book**. Now think of some chores you can do around the house to help Daddy. Write a different chore on each page of the coupon book. Here are some ideas of chores you can do, or you can ask your mommy for ideas, too.

1. **Take out the trash**
2. **Pick up my toys**
3. **Load the dishwasher**
4. **Unload the dishwasher**
5. **Rake the leaves**
6. **Take Abby for a walk**
7. **Sweep the sidewalk**
8. **Vacuum the living room**
9. **Help wash the car**
10. **Put out food and water for Abby**

Place the Coupon Book inside a special card made for Daddy. Give the card to Daddy when he gets home from work.

Chapter 5
I'm Scared!

Game Ideas

The Tray

People: Variable or teams

Goal: Cooperation, Thinking, Remembering

Time: 5 - 10 mins

Materials: 1 tray, towel or cloth, 10-20 small objects, pen and paper per player/team

Method:

- This game can be played as individuals or teams.
- Place all the objects onto the tray. The objects should be small things you can find around the house (scissors, cello tape, biscuit, pin, marble, etc.).
- Place cloth over the objects and place tray in front of everyone.
- Explain that you will uncover the tray for 1 minute, and then the tray will be taken away. It is the player's job to remember as many objects as possible in that time and write them all down.
- The person or team that has the most items listed wins the game. Each person can take turns putting different items on the tray for everyone to guess.

The Chain Gang

People: Variable

Goal: Fun

Time: 5 - 15 mins

Materials: Lots and lots of paperclips

Method:

- This game can be played in teams or individually.
- Dump a huge pile of paperclips in the middle of a circle.
- You give everyone a minute (or more if you wish) to chain together as many paperclips as possible. The winner is the person or team with the largest chain.
- A good game for best out of 3 or 5. At the end of the game you can link all paperclip chains together to see how long the chain is.

Additional Details:
If you don't have paperclips you can make daisy chains or use Lego bricks.

Add A Part

People: Variable

Goal: Fun

Time: 5-20 minutes

Materials: Drawing paper for each person. Pencils with erasers

Method:

- Everyone draws a head on the top part of a piece of paper
- Next step is to fold it over (so tiny bit of neck is showing) & pass it on.
- Next person draws a body, folds & passes it on.
- Next person draws legs, folds & passes it on.
- Finally, the last person draws feet, and passes it back to first person.
- Open up the sheet to see what you've got.

Chapter 7
God, I Need You!

Basic Airplane Folding Instructions

There are so many different types of paper airplanes you can make. The best ones are found on the internet at a very good website for the flyers of paper airplanes. Open the following website: www.amazingpaperairplanes.com and have loads of fun making and flying paper airplanes!

Chapter 8
Who Are My Friends?

10 Reasons Why I Love My Daddy

Here are some suggestions for your child's letter. Help your child to think of reasons they can write in their letter.

1. **You love me!**
2. **You ride bikes with me!**
3. **You clap when I play soccer!**
4. **You take me to the park!**
5. **You play trucks with me!**
6. **You sing with me!**
7. **You take me fishing!**
8. **You found Abby for us!**
9. **You are a good Marine!**
10. **You love Mommy!**
11. **You mow the lawn!**

Chapter 9
I Am God's Child!

This Is Who I Am

I Am Chosen - Ephesians 1:4 - I am chosen by God, holy and without fault in His eyes.

I Am Important - John 1:12 - I have been rightly called a child of God.

I Am Forgiven - Hebrews 10:17 - God no longer remembers my sins.

I Am Valued - Jeremiah 31:3 - God loves me with an everlasting love.

I Am Accepted - Romans 5:8 - I am accepted by Christ.

I Am Powerful - 2 Timothy 1:7 - God has given me the spirit of power, love and a sound mind.

I Am Lovable - Romans 8:38,39 - I am loved by God and nothing will keep us apart.

I Am Connected - Galatians 3:26 - I am a member of God's eternal family.

Chapter 10
Should I Pray?

Levi's Prayer List

1. Dear God, we pray our daddies know You. Help them see they need You every day. Give them good friends to pray with them. Thank You for our great daddies. Amen
2. Dear God, keep our daddies strong when there is danger. We ask You to protect them at all times. Give them wisdom when they need it. Heal them where there is pain. Amen
3. Dear God, we pray our daddies look to You for strength. Heal their broken hearts. Give them courage to make good choices. Help them see how much You love them. Amen
4. Dear God, we pray our daddies will be good leaders in what they do. Keep their minds thinking good thoughts. Keep them on the path to truthfulness in all things. Amen
5. Dear God, help our daddies grow strong in understanding who Jesus is. Keep them strong against evil. Help our daddies ask forgiveness from God about any sin in their lives. Amen

"Thank You For All Your Hard Work" card instructions

To make a nice "Thank You" card use a size $8\frac{1}{2}$" x 11" card stock paper and fold in half so it looks like a card you get for your birthday. On the front write the words "Thank You For All Your Hard Work" using a colored pencil or marker. Open the card and draw your daddy doing his work. Let everyone in the family add their own drawing and sign the card. Put the card some place where he will be surprised when he finds it. Don't forget to give him an extra long hug!

Chapter 11
How Can We Help Daddy?

Ideas for **"We're Proud of You Because ..."** cards: Cut up two $8\frac{1}{2}$" x 11" sheets of card stock into 6 equal parts after folding the sheets in half and then divide into three sections each measuring approximately $2\frac{3}{4}$" x $5\frac{1}{2}$" so you end up with 12 cards. On each card decorate and write out **We're proud of you because (insert one of the ideas below or one of your own ideas)**.

Put one in Daddy's lunch bag or in his shoes the night before. Tape one to the mirror after he goes to bed or tape to the steering wheel of his car. Use your imagination for more ways to show Daddy how proud you are of him.

- **You serve our country!**
- **You give us rides to soccer practice!**
- **You like to study to make yourself better!**
- **You read us stories!**
- **You teach us about cars!**
- **You work out every day so you can be strong!**
- **You cook us hamburgers on the grill!**
- **You help us to get our homework done!**
- **You can juggle three balls!**
- **You take us camping!**

Chapter 12

How Can We Help Each Other?

Use an $8\frac{1}{2}$" x 11" or larger piece of paper and decorate using colorful markers or crayons. Have the words in capital letters stand out with a contrasting color. If you have room on your poster, write out the verse under each promise. Decorate nicely. If you can, place in a frame and gift wrap for Daddy to open on a special occasion.

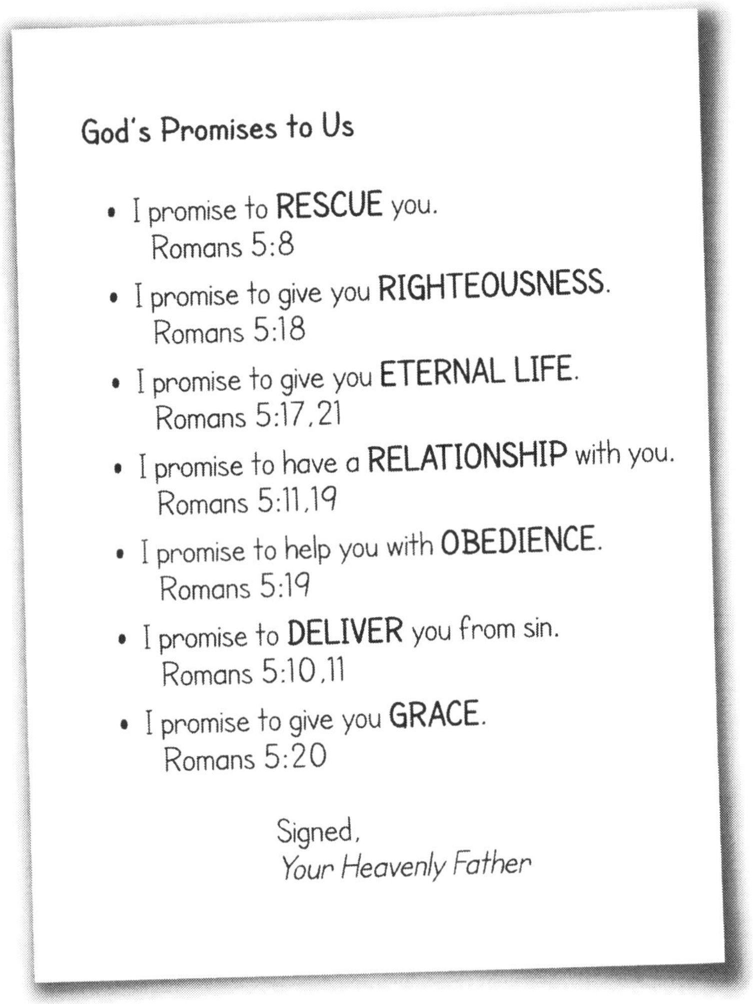

God's Promises to Us

- I promise to **RESCUE** you.
  Romans 5:8
- I promise to give you **RIGHTEOUSNESS**.
  Romans 5:18
- I promise to give you **ETERNAL LIFE**.
  Romans 5:17,21
- I promise to have a **RELATIONSHIP** with you.
  Romans 5:11,19
- I promise to help you with **OBEDIENCE**.
  Romans 5:19
- I promise to **DELIVER** you from sin.
  Romans 5:10,11
- I promise to give you **GRACE**.
  Romans 5:20

Signed,
Your Heavenly Father

Chapter 13
Where Are We Going?

Songs

This Little Light of Mine

Written By: Unknown

This little light of mine,
I'm going to let it shine.
This little light of mine,
I'm going to let it shine.
This little light of mine,
I'm going to let it shine,
Ev'ry day, ev'ry day,
Ev'ry day, ev'ry day,
Gonna let my little light shine.

On Monday, He gave me the gift of love;
On Tuesday, peace came from above;
On Wednesday, told me to have more faith;
On Thursday, gave me a little more grace;
On Friday, told me to watch and pray;
On Saturday, told me just what to say;
On Sunday, gave the power divine,
Just to let my little light shine.

This little light of mine,
I'm going to let it shine.
This little light of mine,
I'm going to let it shine.
This little light of mine,
I'm going to let it shine,
Ev'ry day, ev'ry day,
Ev'ry day, ev'ry day,
Gonna let my little light shine.

I've Got the Joy, Joy, Joy, Joy

Written by: George Willis Cooke
Copyright: Unknown

I've got the joy, joy, joy, joy
Down in my heart! (Where?)
Down in my heart! (Where?)
Down in my heart!
I've got the joy, joy, joy, joy
Down in my heart
Down in my heart to stay.

And I'm so happy
So very happy
I've got the love of Jesus in my heart
Down in my heart
And I'm so happy
So very happy
I've got the love of Jesus in my heart.

I've got the love of Jesus, love of Jesus
Down in my heart (Where?)
Down in my heart! (Where?)
Down in my heart!
I've got the love of Jesus, love of Jesus
Down in my heart (Where?)
Down in my heart to stay.

And I'm so happy
So very happy
I've got the love of Jesus in my heart
Down in my heart
And I'm so happy
So very happy
I've got the love of Jesus in my heart.

I've got the peace that passes understanding
Way down in the depths of my heart!
(Where?)
Down in the depths of my heart!
(Where?)
Down in the depths of my heart!
I've got the peace that passes understanding
Way down in the depths of my heart!
Down in my heart to stay.

And I'm so happy
So very happy
I've got the love of Jesus in my heart
Down in my heart
And I'm so happy
So very happy
I've got the love of Jesus in my heart.

And if the Devil doesn't like it
He can sit on a tack! (Ouch!)
Sit on a tack! (Ouch!)
Sit on a tack!
And if the Devil doesn't like it
He can sit on a tack! (Ouch!)
Sit on a tack to stay!

And I'm so happy
So very happy
I've got the love of Jesus in my heart
Down in my heart
And I'm so happy
So very happy
I've got the love of Jesus in my heart.

Parent's Pages

- Information about the Key Words in each chapter to aid in teaching about Combat Trauma or PTSD/TBI
- Additional resources and websites for each chapter

Chapter 1
What Happened To My Daddy

COMBAT — *Give an analogy of two teams playing against each other in a sport.* Both sides want to win. Each has a different idea of how to win and why they should win. In war, each side thinks they should be the strongest and make the other side try to feel weak. Those who serve in the military from the USA are available to be in combat with many different countries in order to keep our country free. Being in combat all day, every day, can be stressful.

ENEMY — Because the USA believes so strongly in freedom, we call those who do not agree our enemies. Those who are trying to keep anyone from having a free country can be considered an enemy of free people. Bad people in the war set bombs, shoot guns and try to cause confusion. Those who fight for freedom must be careful every hour of every day.

FEAR — An emotion such as fear can be real or imagined. Memories of danger or evil they once experienced can bring back fear over and over again. Sometimes our military have to fight our enemies on little sleep, and after many days and nights with little sleep, they can get stressed. Those coming back from war need time to realize the enemy is no longer after them.

FEELINGS — Everyone has many different types of feelings all day long. When someone is suffering from some type of trauma, the feelings will often be sad. Many, who fight in a war, go through dramatic experiences that bring on deep feelings of despair. It will take time for their minds and emotions to heal from their bad experiences.

PAIN — Getting wounded in the war can be in the body, in the mind and in the heart. Some wounds in the body can be healed with surgery and medicine. Wounds in the mind take time for the healing to occur because the mind keeps recalling what happened. The heart can be healed with lots of patience and caring from families and friends who love those who are suffering.

Additional Resource on COMBAT:
"Down Range: To Iraq and Back"
by Bridget C. Cantrell, Ph.D, and Chuck Dean [WordSmith Publishing, 2005]

Chapter 2
What Am I Doing Wrong, Daddy?

SADNESS — There are many reasons a person will feel sadness. Watching a movie where someone gets hurt or dies can cause sadness. Another example is when someone you love is discouraged and unhappy. There is also a deep sadness when men and women who have fought in a war have seen a close friend die in the war. It takes time for this kind of sadness to heal.

CONFUSION — A child can be confused by adults who don't take the time to explain why something is happening a certain way. A young child in a military family whose parent has fought in a war will not understand what that parent has experienced. It is important that the atmosphere of the home be as positive as possible.

SUFFER — Young children will have a difficult time understanding the suffering of a parent who has symptoms of PTSD/TBI because the wounds are not visible. It is important to explain there are wounds inside the body that need time to heal just as a broken arm or leg needs time to heal inside a cast before it can be used properly again.

ANGER — A child should learn that sometimes their behavior can trigger bad memories from the war for the person who has PTSD/TBI. For instance, a child running through the house yelling at the top of his voice could be such a trigger. Coach the young one to have outside behavior and inside behavior especially until the reintegration into normal family life has been achieved.

BATTLE — Children's cartoons show bad guys and good guys. Movies usually depict characters who do not have good behavior. Children can have an understanding of a battle but only in the context of their experience. As children sense there is a battle going on with a parent who is different after deployment, it may seem confusing to them. Explain there are some battles going on inside of a person no one can really see.

Additional Resource on TRAUMA:
"Veterans and Families' Guide to Recovering from PTSD"
by Stephanie Laite Lanham [Purple Heart Service Foundation, 2007, www.purpleheartfoundation.org or e-mail phsf@purpleheartfoundation.org].

Chapter 3
Why Are Daddy And I So Sad?

LOVE — Children love to get affection from their parents. When a parent tends to hold back affection, children will feel that the parent no longer loves them. One of the symptoms of PTSD can be isolation. It is important to relay to children, who notice the suffering parent is not the same after they return from the latest separation, that they are still loved very much.

LOSS — Part of growing up is to experience all types of situations. Children have to be nurtured and cared for during all the positive and negative times. Having a parent be totally different when they return from combat can be traumatic. There is definitely a sense of loss, but children will not be able to understand why they feel sad. It is the healthy parent's job to help a child mature through all of the experiences. Having a family journal is one idea. When speaking to your child, you can ask, for example, "How does this make you feel?" The comments can be written down in a journal. Each member of the family can contribute especially when the children are too young to write their feelings down.

BURDEN — When a burden seems heavy for an adult to carry, imagine how heavy it seems to a young child. It would be so good to find a group of friends, family, small group members from church, a chaplain or counselors who would help to carry the load with you while you parent your child(ren) as your spouse heals from combat trauma. Being friends with spouses from the same unit can be helpful because you will have experienced the same separation and reintegration issues. Being surrounded by positive and supportive people who can help carry the burden is crucial for children.

SORROW — Because of the uncertainty that can occur in a family setting with a parent who has PTSD/TBI symptoms, children can experience secondary traumatic stress. They may go through several stages of grief due to sorrow because their parent is not what they expected upon return after the long separation. Be sure to speak with someone who can help your children if some of the stages of grief linger.

IDEAS — Talk about ideas of what to do to help Daddy or Mommy get better. Children need to know there is hope for a brighter future, but just as a broken leg takes time to heal, the broken emotional part of a body takes time to heal too. A daily action could be to pray for progress and give it all to God each day, praying that healing will take place.

Additional Resource on GRIEF:

"My Book About the War and Terrorism - A Guided Activity Workbook for Children, Families and Teachers to Encourage Healthy Expression, Learning and Coping"
by Gilbert Kliman, M.D., Harriet Wolfe, M.D., Edward Oklan, M.D., M.P.H.
[The Children's Psychological Health Center, Inc., 2003]

Chapter 4
Should I Say "I'm Sorry"?

WOUND — Sometimes the wounds of the heart cause anger at any moment. Children should be reassured after witnessing an angry outburst that they did not cause the angry words. It is good to have a family plan when a wounded parent acts out with loud regrettable words aimed at someone in the family. The plan should include a gathering of all members of the family and a four-step action taken. 1) Realize the wounded party really does not want to get angry. 2) Pray a prayer similar to this one: "Lord, we choose to forgive our loved one. Help our family heal and get better today and always." 3) Ask God to help everyone in the family to love in spite of angry words that hurt. 4) Decide what kind of love action is needed and from whom.

WEAK — When a student is weak in a subject such as reading, a tutor giving one-on-one help can provide needed strength to continue on the path to reading at grade level or beyond. A weakened emotional state needs some one-on-one tutoring to get through the difficult adjustments that are needed to get well. The strong parent can be that tutor or a professional, who has the ability to work swiftly to focus on the meaningful issues leading to healing and should be called on for help.

STRONG — Most of us, when confronted with a problem, try to solve it ourselves with no outside help. We can definitely have more power when we call upon God to help us through our struggles. It is important to show everyone in the family how to call upon God for all the times we throw our hands up in despair. God is there 24/7 to comfort and to answer prayer.

FORGIVE — Practice forgiveness daily during a time of healing from PTSD/TBI behavior, rather than let it pile up to the point of explosion. The Bible teaches forgiveness should be practiced "seventy times seven" times (Matthew 18:21,22). Remember God has forgiven us our sins, so we should be kind to one another, tender-hearted and forgive each other whenever needed (Ephesians 4:32).

CHOOSE — In the process of a family healing from the trauma of PTSD/TBI symptoms, choices have to be made each day about how to react to what that day holds. No one is perfect, so grace and patience should be extended all around in the midst of healing for the whole family. Each person in the family can act out of character at various times, and all should show patience and care, no matter what.

Additional Resource on FORGIVENESS:
"When You Can't Say 'I Forgive You'"
by Grace Ketterman & David Hazard [NavPress, 2000]

Chapter 5
I'm Scared!

RAGE — Symptoms of grief can include screaming for no reason, slamming doors, kicking things, punching walls or doors, throwing things and just being mean. Grief is part of the process of healing from trauma of any kind. Sometimes it feels better after ranting and raving, but sometimes it doesn't. These sorts of reactions make up rage.

TENSION — It is difficult to trust someone with erratic behavior, especially for a child. The confusion can lead to acting-out behaviors. The healthy parent must be alert to a child's reaction to the tension exhibited in the home because of inappropriate behaviors of the other parent. Some boundaries must be established and, when those lines are crossed, the healthy parent must take action. Any continued angry outbursts and behavior must be stopped even if the one suffering from PTSD has to move out for a time in order to get help on the road to recovery.

ABUSE — Abuse takes many forms: spiritual, emotional, sexual, verbal, psychological and physical. Many PTSD sufferers have had some history of abuse but have ignored it as an adult. It may take a longer time to heal if the abuse experienced while growing up is not dealt with as well. Getting professional help is critical to the complete healing for the family. Allowing abusive behavior to slide does not do anyone any good.

SAFETY — A child will feel unsafe if he witnesses strange behaviors in a parent who has just returned from deployment. A healthy parent can go to the other parent and say, "I've noticed you have no patience with our children and when you get angry, they do not feel safe. I want to ask you to not yell or act so angry. When their noise level or actions irritate you, please walk out of the room, and I will handle the children. If you are not willing to do that, we will leave the house and do something without you until you feel better. Is this agreeable with you?"

HELPERS — Be proactive in setting up a task group around you for escape in case of an emergency. Have a plan worked out with a friend you can call day or night in case you need her or him. Have a packed bag for each member of the family that is only to be grabbed if there is danger. Have a support system set up in case you need to evacuate your home at the drop of a hat. Please don't be shy in reaching out and getting help.

Additional Resource on BOUNDARIES:
"Boundaries in Marriage"
by Dr. Henry Cloud and Dr. John Townsend [Zondervan, 1999]

Chapter 7
God, I Need You!

PROMISE — The amazing part of God's character is that He keeps the promises He makes to His chosen people. Because of human nature, people tend to break promises all the time, but not God. One of the greatest promises God ever made to His people is to save us through Jesus Christ. Those who commit their lives to God through Jesus are assured that they truly are one of God's chosen people. It does not matter how old people are when they ask Jesus into their hearts. He hears, He accepts and loves them immediately.

DISOBEY — People can disobey God's ways. We can think and say and do things God tells us not to do and this would be sinning against Him. The goal is to ask God for forgiveness when we realize we have sinned. God loves to help us be better people every day.

RESCUE — Just like a fireman runs into a burning building to rescue someone from death, Jesus rescues us from the uncertainty that life can have without Him. It is important to read the Bible and study it regularly, to have fellowship with other Christians, to go to church, to memorize verses that are meaningful to you and to pray. God takes the time to help us grow in our knowledge of Him so that when we get stuck, we know we can trust in Him as He rescues us from the little and big things troubling us.

CHOICE — Every day we make choices that can affect us for a lifetime. When we don't know what to do, words from the Bible can give us some answers. Five important elements nurture a new believer in making good choices: **The Holy Spirit** is the power source. **The Word of God** is divine nourishment. **Prayer** is communication with God. **Christian Community** gives us encouragement. **Mindset** is having righteous thoughts such as courage, truth, gratitude, forgiveness and joy.

TRUST — It is so important to find a trusted friend who has a close relationship with God to recommend some good books to read. The more a person can educate themselves on Christian ideals and values and get some feedback for the specific situation, the better. The more love and acceptance given to the one suffering with Combat Trauma symptoms, the closer the family will be to healing. The more awareness there is for all members of the family, the more trust each will have with each other in spite of what happens on a daily basis.

Additional Resource on TRUST:
"Hinds' Feet on High Places"
by Hannah Hurnard [Tyndale House Publishers, 1975]

Chapter 8
Who Are My Friends?

FRIEND — There are people in our lives who want to come alongside us whenever we need help. Having friends at a good church goes a long way in making the whole family feel loved and safe. Friends who have faith want to bear one another's burdens. They are humble and gentle, caring and compassionate. Be ready to receive their help, for it will encourage them to know they can be a bridge to healing for your family.

KINDNESS — For a kind person, it is more about the other person than themselves. There are many reasons a kind person is willing to reach out to someone in need. Those who have the love of Jesus in their lives cannot keep it bottled up inside. They naturally want to give kindness to those around them. The more that is given, the more is received, and thus more is given to even more people. It can be catching.

PATIENT — Although families try to be patient, there can be a point when the family of someone exhibiting PTSD/TBI symptoms must call the professionals. Some of the signs can be the inability to do the job required, not being able to keep food down or eating erratically, not sleeping or sleeping to escape life, losing interest in normal everyday activities, not dressing properly, letting the house become messy and staying that way, and isolating oneself. Ensure everyone in the family is safe. GET HELP NOW!!

MAD — A normal reaction for a person who needs help but doesn't want that help could be anger. However, a caring person who is consistently gentle yet encouraging can be a lifesaver. Hopefully, the one who does not want help will be open to a corrective influence which will help healing take place not only in that person but in the whole family living with PTSD/TBI.

SUFFER — The wound from Combat Trauma or PTSD could be called a wound of the soul or a wound of the mind. Some call it a wound of the identity, since so much of what a suffering person used to think was true about himself has been destroyed. But the wound is just as bad as that of an amputee and needs healing just as badly. It takes an understanding person to be there every step of the healing process.

Additional Resource on PTSD/TBI:

"When War Comes Home: Christ-centered Healing for Wives of Combat Veterans"
by Chris Adsit, Rahnella Adsit & Marshéle Carter Waddell
[Military Ministry Press, 2008]

Chapter 9
I Am God's Child!

Note: There are only five words on the list of Key Words on page 25. But the whole list of truths about who I am (see page 42) contains all eight of these words.

CHOSEN — "Therefore, as God's choice, holy and loved, put on compassion, kindness, humility, gentleness, and patience." Colossians 3:12
(Are we measuring up to good choices leading us to good values?)

IMPORTANT — "Dear friends, now we are God's children, and it hasn't yet appeared what we will be. We know that when he appears we will be like him because we'll see him as he is." 1 John 3:2
(Are we willing to trust God's way is the best way?)

FORGIVEN — "But if we confess our sins, he (God) is faithful and just to forgive us our sins and cleanse us from everything we've done wrong." 1 John 1:9
(Are we keeping our relationship with God sweet because we regularly practice confessing our sins to Him?)

VALUED — "...the Lord appeared to them from a distance: I have loved you with a love that lasts forever. And so with unfailing love, I have drawn you to myself." Jeremiah 31:3
(Are we praising God for drawing us to Him?)

ACCEPTED — "Accept one another, then, just as Christ accepted you, in order to bring praise to God." Romans 15:7 (NIV)
(Are we resting in the fact that we are welcomed and acceptd by Christ?)

POWERFUL — "God didn't give us a spirit that is timid but one that is powerful, loving, and self-controlled." 2 Timothy 1:7
(Are we willing to trust God in the battles we face?)

LOVABLE — "I'm convinced that nothing can separate us from God's love in Christ Jesus our Lord: not death or life, not angels or rulers, not present things or future things, not powers or height or depth, or any other thing that is created." Romans 8:38,39
(Are we taking all our cares to God because He loves us so much?)

CONNECTED — "You are all God's children through faith in Christ Jesus." Galatians 3:26
(Are we remembering to give God the glory because He adopted us?)

Additional Resource:
"CEB (Common English Bible) Deep Blue Kids Bible"
[Common English Bible, 2011]

Chapter 10
Should I Pray?

PRAYER — Talking with God in prayer is vital in our relationship with Him. As we pray, we understand better that it is not words that matter but the communication that counts. When we sense He is listening to us and answering our prayers, we are even more eager to talk with God. God is available all the time, and as we spend time in prayer each day, we will increasingly feel His love, power and influence.

DANGER — It is good practice to pray on a daily basis for those in the military who are in harm's way. Children will love being a part of the prayer time. Praying regularly as a family, especially during a deployment, creates a good habit, that, when encouraged and nurtured, will carry over into adult life. "If you remain in me (Jesus) and my words remain in you, ask for whatever you want and it will be done for you" (John 15:7).

PROTECT — It is built into the military mindset to protect those who serve by your side, especially in combat situations. It is also a parental instinct to protect the children in the family. Children feel secure when they know they are safe. God is also in the business of protecting us when we acknowledge we need His help and call out for it. Families do not have to feel isolated when the enemy of God, Satan, tries to keep a family from making progress toward healing. God is always available.

STRENGTH — When we feel the most vulnerable, we should turn to prayer for strength from the Lord to resist all that is before us. A parent going through PTSD/TBI symptoms will try very hard to go it alone. Without God's interventions moment by moment, it will be a tough road to travel to that ultimate goal of 100% healing. Deliberately submitting to God, resisting Satan's tricks and drawing near to God will work miracles. Satan will see that fervent prayers calling upon a trustworthy God work every time. He will flee.

FORGIVENESS — God is always available to hear us asking for forgiveness when a wrong against another member has been committed. One of the steps toward healing for the whole family is asking forgiveness from God and then the family member. Asking forgiveness from a spouse and the children who have felt betrayed or made to feel insecure because of erratic behavior can bring about an enormous amount of healing. Trusting God for the healing and growth toward a stronger faith is a good step toward demonstrating repentance.

Additional Resources on SPIRITUAL WARFARE:

"The Spiritual Warrior's Prayer Guide"
by Quin Sherrer and Ruthanne Garlock [Servant Publications, 1992]

"A Woman's Guide to Spiritual Warfare"
by Quin Sherrer and Ruthanne Garlock [Servant Publications, 1991]

Chapter 11
How Can We Help Daddy?

CHANGE — The reality of life is that changes are going to come. How a person deals with these changes is important to the health of a family. Healing will go forward on a sooner-rather-than-later basis when the healthy spouse seeks to understand. Having an aware support system in place for the recovering spouse and parent is crucial for the whole family. It is not going to be an easy road but will be very rewarding when progress is seen. What may seem impossible today because of the dynamics of the family could become possible the next day. Don't give up.

EMOTIONS — All family members will be emotionally involved in the healing process. Children should be made to feel just as important as the one being loved and cared for. During the deployment, everyday life was experienced without Daddy and adjustments made. Since Daddy has returned, a new element has been added not only because of his return, but also because he is different than before. Everyone's emotional health should be considered.

HEALING — A healthy atmosphere will aid in the healing process. Keeping the communication channels open is important. Everyone deserves to be heard and to hear what the other person says. When there is a sense of understanding and being understood, everyone in the family will benefit. Adults also need to be willing to ask for help when they are not seeing progress in healing. The afflicted person will only see healing start when they are willing to reach out for help.

ARGUE — It is important to understand what triggers cause arguments to explode. Each person will react differently so a note should be made when things get out of hand. Some types of triggers could be about money, kids, in-laws, work, awareness of spouse's needs, household chores, social functions, communication style and more. It is crucial for parents to keep arguments to themselves and not involve the children in any way. As much as possible, the resolution to a disagreement should be talked out in a civil manner and in private.

DEPLOY — The time away from home for any spouse will require a time of reentry into the family's schedule. The healthy spouse should be sensitive in allowing time for an adjustment without very high expectations. It is important to focus on re-engaging on all aspects after a deployment for all members of the family, no matter what age they are. Consider joining up with a few other couples and go through "The Combat Trauma Healing Manual" by Chris Adsit [Military Ministry Press, 2008] together in a small group setting. This manual provides discussion points about the deployment and seeing how God enters the healing process for maximum success.

The Letter

Here is a copy of the letter sent home to Mommy after a special speaker from the base came and spoke to the children in Cody's class.

Dear Wives of Active Duty Military,

When our military personnel come back from deployment, there can be symptoms resulting from Combat Trauma that could show up soon after returning home or even months later. We want to give you every opportunity to have information that will aid you and your family. Here are some of the symptoms:

Cognitive Symptoms:
Confusion, Forgotten appointments, Decreased self-esteem, Nightmares, Guilt, Shame, Anger, Rage, Helplessness

Emotional Symptoms:
Sadness, Depression, Hypersensitivity, Emotional roller-coaster, Overwhelmed, Bottled-up emotions

Behavioral Symptoms:
Clingy, Impatient, Irritable, Moody, Withdrawn, Sleep disturbances, Substance abuse, Compulsiveness

Physical Symptoms:
Shock, Sweating, Rapid Heartbeat, Breathing difficulties, Aches and pains, Dizziness, Poor self-care

Interpersonal Symptoms:
Feeling vulnerable or unsafe, Decreased interest in intimacy or sex, Mistrust, Suspicious of others, Isolation from friends, Need to control others, Changes in parenting

Spiritual Symptoms:
Doubt concerning one's values or beliefs, Feeling angry or bitter toward God, Feeling far from God, Unloved, Abandoned, Questioning the meaning of life

These are just a few of some of the problems you may see in your loved one suffering from Combat Fatigue or Trauma. Another way of expressing these symptoms is called Post-Traumatic Stress (PTS). Realize that if your loved one has not reached out to anyone for help, there are many who want to help your family get the help you need.

Don't hesitate to call the Chaplain, the Family Readiness Officer or someone you know who can become a Battle Buddy with your family. Seek the help you need in order for the healing to take place for everyone.

Sincerely,
Chaplain Hunt

Additional Resource on CONFLICTS:
"The Seven Conflicts"
by Tim and Joy Downs [Moody Publishers, 2003]

Chapter 12
How Can We Help Each Other?

DEPRESSED — Mothers who are married to Combat Trauma sufferers need to be pro-active about protecting their children from unintended damage. A child who does not get emotional support throughout the healing process of a parent could become depressed, have problems at school, or have anxious thoughts. It is so important to keep a watchful eye on each of the children in the family for any signs of secondary effects from the Combat Trauma symptoms exhibited by the family member who is in post-deployment.

TRAUMA — Young children can be affected by traumatic events, so parents should be on the alert for any unusual behavior. When there is chaos in the home, children and the healthy spouse could develop secondary traumatization which adds a hurdle to the healing process. Professional help should be called on to sort out a plan to get everyone on the right track. If nothing is done, the ramifications could lead to young people not having good coping skills for the trials of life. Please do not be afraid to ask for help.

UNDERSTAND — Children need to know how to deal with some of the common characteristics of those with Combat Trauma or PTSD/TBI. They could include hyper-vigilance, exaggerated startle response, fight or flight reactions, flashbacks, etc. Help them understand they will need to show patience toward Daddy by letting them know he had to be alert at all times while he was at war. He had to be sure that he and all of his men who were fighting the enemy would stay alive. It was so important for him to be ready for anything to happen. Since he has been home, he has had a hard time not thinking this way. Help the children help Daddy by being as calm as possible when he is trying to remember he is not at war anymore.

TRUTH — It is good to give an accurate picture of what is happening in the family as the healing process takes place. It's okay to let your child know how you, as the healthy parent, feel about what is happening, but be careful not to scare or alarm a child. Explain that what is happening in the war is real—unlike violent movies, cartoons, video games or television programs. Help your child to understand that during war, real people are involved and some may die or get hurt. Also explain that some of the injuries are to the body, and some are to the emotions.

BROKEN — Some families have to face the drama caused by Combat Trauma for a long time. This seemingly never-ending experience can cause hearts to give up. The stresses of life can break you! But it takes God's love, mercy, kindness, compassion and strength to build you back up. The brokenhearted can be mended with a plan that includes God's love, the support of Christians who can relate and mentor those who are hurting and the fellowship of the church body. A suffering family can go from heartache to hope in the future when God gets involved!

Additional Resources on FAMILY TRAUMA:

"My Book About the War and Terrorism - A Guided Activity Workbook for Children, Families and Teachers to Encourage Healthy Expression, Learning and Coping"
by Gilbert Kliman, M.D., Harriet Wolfe, M.D., Edward Oklan, M.D., M.P.H.
[The Children's Psychological Health Center, Inc., 2003]

"Why Is Daddy Like He Is?"
by Patience Mason [Patience Press, 1992]

Chapter 13
Where Are We Going?

TRANSFORM — If the symptoms of Combat Trauma continue to cause problems, then something has to change. A good sit-down with your spouse to analyze where you are, what the future looks like and how to get there will benefit every member of the family. Being serious about healing will bring hope.

DREAM — Believing there will be an end to the trauma can be a healthy attitude. Each member of the family can have a part in expressing what they dream it will be like to have fun again and to be together without drama. It will take courage for everyone to believe their lives will have normalcy to them. There may be adjustments to what normal is now. Maybe changing locations or jobs would be helpful. Maybe changing the type of friends to hang out with would help. Everyone should think positively on getting through, on letting God help, and being open to changes which may need to be made.

DEPEND — The hardest part of recovery is asking for help. For the healthy spouse, knowing when to realize something is not right is important. There are many sources of aid through the military, through the chaplain, through the local churches and through friends who have successfully seen healing take place in their own lives. For the one going through the combat trauma, it is also important to know when the problems are too big to handle. When life does not seem to ever get back to normal during the post-deployment, it is time to ask for help. Before giving up altogether and doing something drastic like walking out on the family, getting lost in drugs, alcohol and sex, or other activities causing anxiety for everyone, ask for help.

GOAL — Setting some measurable goals regarding work environment, relationship building, location, finances, diet and exercise, medical issues, excesses or other pertinent goals will go a long way on getting on the right track for the whole family. Having a vision shared by all members of the family will give each one importance in the healing process. God uses all the circumstances people are confronted with, changing them into opportunities to grow in character and trust. Goals are the avenue that keeps everyone on the right track.

HOPE — Keeping a firm grip on faith in God and His healing power to find victory will surely aid while traversing through the rough patches. Where there is brokenness, there will be healing. Where there are wounds, there will be new power. Where there is darkness, there will be light. Let God be the one to give hope that only He can provide. The words of Romans 12:12 in the New Testament ring true: "Be happy in your hope, stand your ground when you're in trouble, and devote yourselves to prayer."

Additional Resources on HEALING:

"The Combat Trauma Healing Manual: Christ-centered Solutions for Combat Trauma"
By Chris Adsit [Military Ministry Press, 2008]

"Courage After Fire"
by Keith Armstrong, L.C.S.W., Suzanne Best, Ph.D., Paula Domenici, Ph.D.
[Ulysses Press, 2006]